Conservation planning in town and country

Conservation planning in town and country

Papers by Robin Bloxsidge, Honor Chapman,
Gerald Dix, Anne Dennier, Laurence Fricker,
John Jones, Ann MacEwen, Josephine Reynolds
and John Nelson Tarn

Edited by Josephine Reynolds

Liverpool University Press

Published by
LIVERPOOL UNIVERSITY PRESS
123 Grove Street, Liverpool L7 7AF

Copyright © 1976 Liverpool University Press

Printed in Great Britain by
Willmer Brothers Ltd, Birkenhead

ISBN 0 85323 393 4

First published 1976

Preface

The University of Liverpool commemorated European Architectural Heritage Year 1975 in two ways. First, in October 1975 an Exhibition was held in the Exhibition Hall in the Senate House of the University entitled *Conservation in an Urban Environment*. The Exhibition consisted of illustrations of conservation work planned and executed by the Metropolitan Districts of Merseyside and Greater Manchester. Also on display were some 150 reports on conservation prepared by local authorities throughout England and Wales.

Secondly, a special issue of the *Town Planning Review* was published to coincide with the Exhibition. This special issue was entirely devoted to aspects of conservation planning. By discussing in a series of related articles the issues and problems of conservation the journal believed it could make a contribution to European Architectural Heritage Year by inviting a number of authors to write on themes which the Editor, after discussion with the authors, thought would bring out the major issues of conservation in the British context. The themes developed by the authors, while reinforcing the aims and objectives underlying the Heritage Year campaign, were nevertheless seen to be of a much more lasting character and were important contributions to the theory and practice of conservation planning. In addition, the important contribution of the local authorities to conservation planning was recognized by the inclusion of the annotated bibliography of conservation reports, which had been on display in the Exhibition. The articles and the bibliography contained in the special issue are published here as a book with minor alterations and additions.

The Editor is most grateful to all the authors who contributed articles—now the chapters of this book—and for their willing help in finding the appropriate photographs and maps to illustrate their material. I am also extremely grateful to Robin Bloxsidge, Editorial Assistant to the *Review* for his contribution, for his careful checking of material and for sending requests to local authorities for their conservation reports and the subsequent handling of the magnificent deluge of material which came as a response to this request. I would also like to thank John Harvey for designing and redrawing maps for the articles and for collating the photographs and assisting with the local authorities' reports.

The Department of Civic Design,
The University of Liverpool.

JOSEPHINE P. REYNOLDS

Notes on Contributors

Robin Bloxsidge
Editorial Assistant of the *Town Planning Review*.

Honor Chapman
Partner in Nathaniel Lichfield and Partners, planning, development, transportation, and economic consultants.

D. Anne Dennier
Lecturer in the Department of Civic Design in the University of Liverpool.

Gerald Dix
Lever Professor of Civic Design in the University of Liverpool.

Laurence J. Fricker
Lecturer in the School of Architecture of Portsmouth Polytechnic.

John M. Jones
Lecturer in the Department of Civic Design in the University of Liverpool.

Ann MacEwen
Consultant in Colin Buchanan and Partners, planning consultants, and a senior lecturer in the School for Advanced Urban Studies in the University of Bristol.

Josephine P. Reynolds
Senior lecturer in the Department of Civic Design in the University of Liverpool and Editor of the *Town Planning Review*.

John Nelson Tarn
Roscoe Professor of Architecture in the University of Liverpool.

Contents

EG's

Introduction

The aims and objectives of conservation
European Architectural Heritage Year 1975

Most people throughout the world and particularly in Europe and the United Kingdom were aware that 1975 was European Architectural Heritage Year. They may have known too that it was in 1972 that the Council of Europe's Committee of Ministers decided formally that 1975 should be designated European Architectural Heritage Year and that the stated aims of the Heritage Year campaign were:

'To awaken the interest of the European peoples in their common architectural heritage;

To protect and enhance buildings and areas of architectural or historic interest;

To conserve the character of old towns and villages;

To assure for ancient buildings a living role in contemporary society'.[1]

The three-year Heritage Year campaign, with its slogan 'A Future for Our Past', was organized by a committee under the Chairmanship of Lord Duncan-Sandys, who is President of Europa Nostra.[2] Although European Architectural Heritage Year was initiated by the Council of Europe, European countries outside the Council were invited to participate in the campaign and to be represented on the Committee. In nearly all the participating countries the campaign was organized by separate national committees administered by government departments. In the United Kingdom the situation was rather different, the campaign being administered by the Civic Trust with financial assistance from the Government.[3,4]

The United Kingdom Council was set up in 1972 under the Presidency of HRH The Duke of Edinburgh, and the Chairman of the Executive Committee of the Council, which included amongst its members the Chairmen of the National Committees for Scotland, Wales and Northern Ireland, was the Countess of Dartmouth. Heritage Year in Britain, although embracing the Council of Europe's aims, was planned on what seemed to be a broader base with continuing conservation as its underlying theme. 'This Council calls upon all those organizations and individuals having a responsibility for the preservation of ancient monuments, historic buildings and areas of historic, architectural or technological interest, to decide upon and to initiate the most appropriate action which needs to be taken in the United Kingdom. In particular, the Council invites the active support and initiative of:

local authorities, upon whose active co-operation the success of the campaign must largely depend;

property owners, from the great estates to the individual householder, with all their special responsibilities;

the voluntary bodies which have been the leaders in this field;

the environmental professions, whose expertise is needed to solve the technical problems;

industry and commerce, as sponsors of development, patrons of the arts and a major influence on the quality of the human environment;

the channels of information and education—press, radio and television;

cultural societies of every kind;

educationists at every level for only through an informed and enthusiastic public can the long-term success of the campaign be assured'.[5]

Whichever way the aims of European Architectural Heritage Year (EAHY) were interpreted, Heritage Year was a most important landmark in European history. The demands of modern society and technology have resulted in building development and land uses which have a scale which is quite out of character with the older fabric of historic towns and countryside. When new development takes place, unless particular care is taken, much of the special character of these older places is destroyed. On the other hand, new building can bring with it the greater convenience of an environment designed for contemporary living. To combine the best of the old with the convenience of the new is one of the major issues of conservation practice. But this would be a gross oversimplification of the problems which have to be solved when a country like Britain, with a marvellous heritage of old and often beautiful buildings and towns and villages set in a countryside of unsurpassed scenery, is faced with the need to introduce new development which could bring with it much economic advantage.

This book explores several themes which have been the basis of the EAHY campaign in Britain. These themes are concerned with the aims and objectives of conservation, the machinery of conservation, planning as an aid to conservation, the conservation of historic gardens and landscapes and the special problems of our small-scale heritage. While each theme is dealt with separately, yet there are several threads running through each theme which are generally common to them all. For example, there is the need to equate the cost of conservation with the value of our heritage to future generations. There is the need to forge closer links between local authorities and private organizations if conservation is to be positive rather than a paper exercise. There is the need, too, to pay special attention to conservation as a means of improving our less well-off areas and to conservation in the more 'ordinary' areas in Britain. In all these themes, too, education, public participation and a sensitive approach to our surroundings are basic to the whole question of what might be called heritage planning.

The Issues and Problems of Conservation

The aims of the campaign for European Architectural Heritage Year (EAHY) provide a good starting point for a discussion on the aims and objectives of conservation. One can discuss, for example, whether the Heritage Year aims were too narrow and confining and may lead to Europe being something of a museum piece even if new uses can be found for old buildings. It can be argued, too, that the aims relate only to physical development and do not take account of the social and economic circumstances of the areas which contain the historic buildings or of the people who live in these areas. It could also be suggested, in appearing to relate the aims solely to historic buildings and historic towns, that places of much less distinction, but for one reason or another seem to give a pleasant environment, should also be included. Do the aims suggest that new buildings should be tomorrow's heritage? Do they even take any account of the necessity for some new buildings in old areas, or are there objections to any new buildings at all? These are some of the thoughts and questions that spring to mind in thinking about the Heritage Year aims. And there are certainly many others.

The essays in this volume develop some of these ideas further, discussing conservation in terms of the different and various constraints likely to affect the initiation and implementation of heritage schemes. Honor Chapman suggests that conservation should be much more closely related to the wider planning and economic systems and that the limited resources available for conservation should be allocated only when adequate analysis reveals that conservation can compete on its own terms with other forms of development. Gerald Dix tends rather to take the opposite view that a fine old city such as Norwich is a priceless asset. Places like Norwich are of national importance and should receive national support and, where the enhancement of environmental quality is concerned, it should be accepted that it might be necessary to pay to retain this quality, not necessarily in financial terms but by accepting limitations, of say, for example, convenient access to buildings, and by not giving way to pressures for new development when this is suggested. On this count, conservation in Norwich, a pioneer city in the preservation of historic buildings and streets, would fulfil very exactly all the Heritage aims. The old city of Chester, however, as Anne Dennier points out in her contribution, has been adapted to deal with modern pressures, especially traffic. Some new buildings there have been so well designed that they act as foils to old buildings and will undoubtedly become part of Chester's heritage of the future on their own account.

The aim of 'assuring for ancient building a living role in contemporary society' is stressed in Ann MacEwen's article on the New Town in Edinburgh and later in John Jones' article on Conwy. There is a difference in context here for Edinburgh's New Town is on an altogether grander scale than Conwy. But the essential conservation aim is the same—to plan for and maintain a 'lived in' quality for the old residential areas that form the major part of the built environment in each place. There is perhaps a closer link between the essay of John Jones and that of John Tarn, where the concept of conservation of 'ordinariness' is discussed in the context of Derbyshire Heritage. Here there is a plea for conservation which recognizes that the best of our heritage is sometimes unspectacular—as are the small houses in Conwy. It is a heritage of vernacular architecture which has relied on local building materials and styles of building developed over thousands of years and is related closely to climate, geology and landscape. It is this kind of ordinary heritage that John Tarn considers should be conserved. But it is probably much more difficult to make a case for this unless the much broader issues of landscape heritage are involved. Here the conservation aims, some people would say, would tend to fall outside those of EAHY but it could well be argued that the architectural heritage of Britain is one of both town and countryside and that the cultural landscapes such as the walled fields of the Derbyshire limestone plateau are indeed part of our national heritage.[6] Fortunately, in Britain, country towns and villages and country houses, estates and parks are so cosely integrated with the landscape that it would be difficult to discuss conservation measures of these without, in many cases, relating them to the surrounding countryside. The essays by Laurence Fricker and John Tarn state this clearly, making a strong case for providing better financial provision for the conservation of historic gardens and of the landscape.

This discussion of the aims of EAHY suggest that the Heritage campaign could have had a much broader base, perhaps recognizing that in many parts of Europe, and, in Britain in particular, quite a number of towns and landscapes, although not outstanding from a historical point of view could nevertheless be classified as worthy of some special attention. It also suggests that in Britain the campaign may not have had the impact that it should have had in persuading the public that besides financial help, encouragement and enthusiasm are needed if the best of the past is to be handed on to future generations.

This implied criticism of the objectives of the campaign is perhaps unfair because as the campain developed it seemed that the issues and problems of conservation were difficult to define, and it may have been necessary to limit the scope of the campaign in order that something could be achieved, as indeed it has been.

Changing Objectives in the Campaign

Reports of the conferences and symposia that were held during the Heritage campaign together with information from Heritage campaign secretariats are a useful source of information about the aims and objectives of conservation.[7] At these meetings several resolutions were passed which revealed the intensity of feeling and the breadth of vision of the delegates and this was undoubtedly the force that was needed to promote a campaign of this size and scope.

THE CAMPAIGN IN EUROPE

In 1963 the parliamentary assembly of the Council of Europe adopted a recommendation for the protection and development of sites and groups of historic buildings and made a resolution defining the special part to be played by local authorities and later, in 1970, a recommendation was made for a law to be passed relating to the protection of the European cultural heritage.

These actions led to the formulation by governments of a Five Year Plan not only to protect monuments and sites but also to proclaim 1975 as a Year 'to be devoted to the defence of European cultural heritage of buildings'. But it is perhaps at the European Symposium of Towns of Historic Interest held in Split in Yugoslavia in October 1971 that the most important resolutions were passed dealing with the aims and objectives of conservation. These resolutions were known as the Split Declaration.[8]

In relation to the role of local authorities and historic towns the Declaration said that the main objective of preservation should be the reanimation of monuments etc., and reanimation operations should be included in local, and even regional development plans where they can serve as stimulants and be carried out through permanent co-operation between all those concerned at different levels. The reanimation plans should be drawn up under the responsibility of local authorities with the help of various specialists—architects, town planners, sociologists and representatives of the areas directly involved. Urban development plans should deal especially with historic streets and develop traffic plans to limit traffic, eliminate car parking and create pedestrian areas. It was emphasized that because preservation and reanimation would pay dividends in the short and long term, Government financial support could be expected. It was further recommended that regional planning and protection of the cultural heritage should be co-ordinated and that national scientific and technical services should be re-designed and given greater power to assist local authorities to carry out their new duties.

The Declaration referred also to the need for public participation in the form of dialogue and educational programmes and the need to train architects, engineers and town planners to carry out plans for reviving and re-integrating ancient buildings and historic sites into a modern urban environment.

The broad and varied aims of conservation that formed the basis of the Declaration are obscured in this too brief synopsis. The move towards the more simple set of general aims came with the launching of European Architectural Heritage Year at a conference in July 1973 in Zurich.

In Zurich these general aims, however, were supported by resolutions which were to be the guidelines for the EAHY campaign and they deserve, like the Split Declaration, a brief comment.[9] There are three of these resolutions— Resolution No. 1, Legislation on the Integrated Protection of Conservation Areas of Cultural Interest; Resolution No. 2, Conservation, Restoration and Rehabilitation of Old Districts; Resolution No. 3, Promotion of Public Interest. While all three resolutions are of great interest we can only be selective here and it is Resolution No. 1 that is most relevant to our discussion. This resolution dealt with the definition of conservation areas saying they should be coherent, compact and of historic, archaeological, artistic, characteristic or picturesque interest. Within these areas there was to be no unauthorized destruction or conversion of buildings and these conservation areas should be integrated into general planning strategies. The objectives of protection within the conservation areas should include the preservation, restoration and enhancement of architectural heritage, and also the rehabilitation of dilapidated areas and their integration in contemporary society. On the financial aspects of conservation the resolution suggested that governments should be invited to set up national funds to commemorate EAHY which could be supplemented by national appeals and public grants. The resolution, however, recognized that the financing of conservation was a most complex problem.

We can see from this summary that the European campaign was now using ideas which had already become facts in Britain because by 1973 the programme of designation of conservation areas in Britain had been well under way since the passing of the Civic Amenities Act in 1967.[10] But before we go on to the British scene we should discuss the Council of Europe's contribution to EAHY—the Pilot Projects.

THE PROGRAMME OF PILOT PROJECTS

The Council of Europe's contribution to EAHY was to select a series of restoration projects which would 'demonstrate what can be done, and with what resources, to save Europe's heritage of fine buildings'.[11] These projects 'are situated in differing regional, urban and rural areas and have been selected as the most significant examples in member countries of integrated conservation'. That is, restoring to a practical use in modern society and integrating into the overall regional or urban plan. There are some 50 of these in 17 member countries and four are in the United Kingdom. These are Chester, Poole, Edinburgh New Town and the National Trust for Scotland's Little Houses Improvement Scheme. Since two essays in this book are devoted to Chester and Edinburgh's New Town we do not need to discuss the Pilot Projects here except that part of the programme of Pilot Projects included the holding of three symposia with on the spot examination of three of the Projects. The first was held in Edinburgh in January 1974,[12] the second in Bologna in October 1974,[13] and the third in Krems in Austria in April 1975.[14] The product of these symposia is relevant to our discussion on conservation aims and objectives.

In these three symposia the emphasis has been on the social and economic implications of conservation although in Edinburgh the quality of the urban environment was discussed in relation to new development. And again it was stressed that the planning process at regional and local level should use both methods to satisfy the changing needs of society. It was also suggested that the Council of Europe should circulate a document illustrating the wide range of new uses for old buildings.

The idea that conservation can keep community and social life together better than new development was stressed but it was felt that preservation should not only be for the privileged but for the poorer sections of the population as well. Lastly it was thought that the most successful schemes were those where there was a high degree of public participation.

The British Contribution

Well before EAHY was proclaimed, the conservation of historic towns and buildings was not just an interesting idea. It was part and parcel of British planning legislation. In her chapter on the machinery of conservation Honor Chapman traces the development of the financial aspects of this legislation from the Ancient Monuments Act of 1913 to the Town and Country Amenities Act 1974. Here, however, we are perhaps more concerned with the conservation aims which led to the first important act—the Civic Amenities Act 1967. This act recognized the importance of the setting of whole groups of buildings of architectural and historic interest and required local authorities to determine which parts of their areas were 'areas of special architectural and historic interest'.

It was during the passage of the Civic Amenities Act that studies were commissioned to examine how conservation policies might be implemented and as a result the Bath, Chester, York and Chichester reports were published.[15] Alongside these studies the government published other studies designed particularly to interest the layman. *Preservation and Change*[16] published in 1967 discussed the need for a conservation policy which would plan preservation and change together so that unwelcome pressure particularly from preservation is diverted and new life brought into old areas. This was followed later by *New Life for Old Buildings* in 1971 which showed practical examples of old buildings being adapted to new uses.[17] These and countless other reports and publications providing an information service for the public and practical propaganda towards developing a comprehensive conservation policy. Much of this persuasion was, of course, instigated by the Civic Trust, the voluntary organization primarily concerned with civic amenities in this country and which, with financial help from the government, has conducted the Heritage Campaign in Britain.

1971 saw the designation of 'conservation areas' in order to 'preserve and enhance their character and appearance'.[18] Further changes in legislation were made in 1974 with the passing of the Town and Country Amenities Act.[19] But just prior to the passing of this Act the Government issued a circular which outlined the responsibilities of local authorities for ensuring that the statutory lists of buildings of architectural and historic interest were complete and dealt with the problem of possible overlaps in the responsibility for the scheduling of ancient monuments and the listing of historic buildings.[20] The circular stressed the continuing need to preserve and find new uses for listed buildings and finally asked local authorities to co-operate in ensuring the local success of European Architectural Heritage Year.

Perhaps even more important the 1974 Act requires local authorities, to formulate and publish, '... proposals for the preservation and enhancement, of any parts of their area which are conservation areas. Moreover, local authorities are required to submit these proposals for consideration to a public meeting and 'have regard to any views concerning the proposals expressed by persons attending the meeting'.[21]

The provisions of the Town and Country Amenities Act form a suitable background to discuss the aims of conservation as they appear to exist in this country at the moment. These aims have undergone changes in emphasis over the past few years and since the start of the major conservation area programme. When the Chichester report was published, for example, the recommendations outlined in the report aimed to adapt the historical parts of the City of Chichester to fulfil present and foreseeable needs in a way that is economically viable, while preserving as much as possible of their existing and attractive environmental quality and enhancing them through whatever adaptations and new developments are considered desirable and appropriate.[22] One could call this a system of adaptation, preservation, and enhancement.

While, obviously these aims are suitable for beautiful towns and cities like Chichester some other criteria were needed to deal with areas of less distinction but with an interesting character and this was recognized by the UK Secretariat when it stressed that campaigns should not be confined to 'showpiece houses and beauty-spot villages'. Almost every city, town, suburb and village in Britain has areas, buildings and features of architectural and historic interest which are worth preserving—and which often need enhancement. Sometimes the very existence of these assets is overlooked, and they need to be brought to light.[23] From this viewpoint a new criterion of selection is emerging. Conservation areas need not necessarily be wholly concerned with an architectural context, and this is recognized in the Town and Country Amenities Act when the question of historic landscapes is catered for. Another change is the emphasis on the need to draw in public opinion as part of the conservation exercise in this way making conservation much more of an 'action' process.

In fact the whole of the EAHY campaign was based on assumptions that it could persuade and attract the public to be active participants in an ongoing programme which would extend beyond 1975. But how far the public can be persuaded to become really enthusiastic about conservation, particularly in the poorer areas of Britain such as, for example, Merseyside and Teesside, and where financial resources are sparse, is a big question.

A NEW SET OF OBJECTIVES

The final stages of the EAHY campaign culminated in the conference held in Amsterdam in October 1975. A joint declaration issued by 29 nations from East and West Europe consolidated and clarified the aims and objectives which had guided the campaign. These objectives, as we have seen, ranged from a desire to protect small monuments to the need to integrate conservation policies into a system of dynamic urban and regional planning. The *Amsterdam Declaration*[24] is based on a series of themes which involve the responsibility of the peoples of Europe to protect their priceless heritage, the need to make architectural conservation an important objective of town and country planning, the use of rehabilitation as a method of avoiding big social changes in older housing areas, and the need to maintain historical continuity as a means of establishing a sense of security in the face of social change. The declaration called for strengthened legislative and administrative measures to protect cities, towns and buildings. It urged governments to give adequate financial assistance to local authorities and to grant financial support and fiscal relief to private owners.

If none of these objectives is particularly new yet the declaration, in spite of the economic climate in which it was issued, should constitute a really good Heritage Charter which will give a renewed impetus to the progress of conservation planning in the future.

Conservation Planning: The Wider Aims

The campaign for EAHY had, in many places in Britain, been carried out with quite astonishing enthusiasm. There was an imaginative series of programmes in schools, together with public lectures, exhibitions, and travel to Heritage Year towns. Town trails now lead enthusiastic sightseers, both young and old, round towns and into interpretation centres. Thousands of conservation areas have been or are in the process of being designated. And if there is something of a suspicion that this is all a vast paper exercise this view is dispelled by the real progress that is being made with the help of Conservation and Heritage Grants for the restoration of many old and historic buildings. It is, of course, unfortunate that Heritage Year has coincided with the economic crisis, but this did not prevent the UK Secretariat from going ahead with its programmes and with the publication of Information and News-sheets. Indeed, as the editor of *Heritage News* pointed out, 'We must look again (we shall have to anyway) at grandiose schemes that make a clean sweep of everything in sight, regardless of its architectural quality and community value'.[25]

Thus economic circumstances are forcing us to regard conservation in a different light. We are beginning to regard our huge building stock not only as our heritage but also as a reservoir of building space to be used more intensively. In doing this we still have to make decisions about whether it is better to spend more on special projects of great historic interest or whether we should spread our limited resources over a greater number of less expensive but worthwhile schemes. These kinds of decisions are relatively easy to make. The great number of conservation areas that have been designated should help, when the analysis of these has been done, to decide where our limited resources should be allocated to produce the greatest benefit. Within the conservation areas there are still difficult decisions to make of whether to restore or whether to redevelop. Still more evidence is needed to measure whether renovation is more economical than redevelopment. And sometimes this economic decision is not the over-riding one. Architectural design in old cities sometimes provides an excellent foil to old buildings and some new buildings are so well designed that they are seen to be the heritage of the future. By allowing some new building to take place, an old less prosperous town is sometimes given new life without its becoming a museum piece.

It is perhaps outside the designated conservation areas that the greatest safeguards have to be established. New industrial building may well be needed to attract employment into the older parts of our cities as well as into the country-side. In the city this development may lie close to conservation areas and bring with it large-scale building in conflict with our heritage areas. Similarly, and there are now numerous cases of this, new agricultural buildings are frequently on the scale and bulk of large factories totally unsuited to their surroundings.[26] We can only indicate briefly that these aims of conservation should not only be directed toward historic buildings in urban areas, but should also be seen in a wider context of our total heritage. It does seem that the *Amsterdam Declaration* goes a long way towards embracing these wider aims and objectives.

B

NOTES AND REFERENCES

1 EAHY 1975, *Aims, Organisations & Activities*, Council of Europe, 1973.

2 EUROPA NOSTRA, an international federation of non-governmental organizations for the protection of Europe's cultural and national heritage.

3 Switzerland's campaign is the only other country where the campaign is being administered by a private society.

4 CIVIC TRUST, 17, Carlton House Terrace, London, SW1Y 5AW. Founded in 1957, the Civic Trust is a recognized charity which encourages the protection of towns and villages.

5 EAHY 1975, Report to the United Kingdom Council, July 1974, United Kingdom Secretariat, and the United Kingdom Declaration, December 1972.

6 *Report of the National Parks Policy Review Committee*, DoE/Welsh Office, HMSO, April 1974.

7 Council of Europe, Secretariat General, Directorate of Press and Information, Strasbourg. United Kingdom Secretariat, European Architectural Heritage Year, 17 Carlton House Terrace, London SW1Y 5AW.

8 Council of Europe, European Symposium of Towns of Historic Interest. *The Split Declaration*, October 1971.

9 Council of Europe, Press Information, The Start of a Campaign to Save Europe's Monuments. Results of Council of Europe Conference held in Zurich in July 1973.

10 The Civic Amenities Act of 1967 imposed a duty on local planning authorities to decide which areas as opposed to buildings are of special architectural significance, the character of which it is desirable to preserve or enhance.

11 EAHY, Information Sheet No. 1, July 1974, United Kingdom Secretariat.

12 Council of Europe, Press Communiqué, *The Social and Economic Implications of Conservation*, Results of The Edinburgh Symposium, January 1974.

13 Council of Europe, Press Communiqué, *The Social Cost of the Conservation of Historic Centres*, Results of the Bologna Symposium, October 1974.

14 Council of Europe, Press Communiqué, *Neither a Slum, Nor a Museum*. Report of the Krems Symposium, April 1975.

15 Esher, Viscount, *York. A Study in Conservation*. MoHLG, HMSO, 1969. Insall, Donald W. and Associates, Chester. *A Study in Conservation*, MoHLG, HMSO, 1969. Buchanan, Colin and Partners, MoHLG, HMSO, 1969. Burrows, G. S., *Chichester. A Study in Conservation*, MoHLG, HMSO, 1969. See also Dennier, D. Anne, Book Review of the Four Studies, *Town Planning Review*, Vol. 41, No. 1, January 1970, pp. 92–97.

16 MoHLG, *Preservation and Change*, HMSO, 1967.

17 MoHLG, *New Life for Old Buildings*, HMSO, 1971.

18 Town and Country Planning Act 1971, Part XV, section 277 (formerly Civic Amenities Act, Part 1, section 1, sub-section 1 (6) of the original Act was amended and transferred to the Town and Country Planning Act, 1971, section 28).

19 Town and Country Amenities Act 1974, 'An Act to make further provision for the control of development in the interests of amenity, for the protection of trees and the preservation of buildings of architectural or historic interest and their surroundings and landscapes, and for related purposes'.

20 Joint Circular, Circular 102/74, Department of the Environment, and Circular 171/74, Welsh Office.

21 Joint Circular, Circular 147/74, Department of the Environment, and Circular 220/74, Welsh Office.

22 Burrows, G. S., op. cit.

23 UK Secretariat, EAHY, Information, July 1974.

24 Council of Europe, Press Communiqué, The *Amsterdam Declaration*, November 1975.

25 UK Secretariat, Heritage Year News, Number Two, 1975.

26 *Twentieth Report of the Royal Fine Art Commission*, January 1966–July 1968, pp. 8–10.

The machinery of conservation

Finance and planning problems

HONOR CHAPMAN

Almost everything which could possibly be said about conservation must surely, by now, have been said. Articles on its varied aspects are legion, both in the technical and the popular press. This chapter was intended to open with words such as 'Conservation appears to be gaining momentum . . .', only to find that Summerson pointed this out in 1947.[1] However, to those whose planning antennae are directed towards this particular wavelength it is clear that, as far as the built environment is concerned, the public view is extending beyond buildings of architectural and historic interest to include others which, on the face of it, embody substantial resources of building materials already assembled to provide floor-space and which offer a type of accommodation which might not be provided on redevelopment. For example, the recent controversy over the proposed redevelopment of Grand Buildings in Trafalgar Square can be cited.[2] The general need to avoid waste of vital scarce resources and to expand the production of oil, agriculture and forestry products are sharpening the conservation issues in the countryside.

Although conservation has been given a specific meaning in planning, it is possible to argue that, for reasons of scarcity of resources, the greater part of planning, as it will need to be practised in the next few years, is conservation in its widest sense. The field is extensive but, for reasons of space, this article is confined to the elements with which European Architectural Heritage Year is concerned: primarily areas of historic, architectural and technological interest, but also ancient monuments and historic buildings. Conservation is taken to mean the making of the best use of the resources embodied in these elements, including their maintenance in a good state of repair; and, in some cases, maintaining other features as well, such as the characteristics of the activities which take place within the buildings, both social and technological; for example, the community of Covent Garden or the Harvey water-pumping engine at East Pool Mine in Cornwall.

Most articles on conservation treat with what is happening to individual buildings or areas and the efforts of different organizations, some take a more synoptic view of a specific aspect such as finance[3] or its rôle in planning.[4] The economics of conservation, both in the general[5] and the particular as related to planning,[6] has also been considered, as has its politics.[7] The attempt is made here to consider not so much what is being done, but the rôles of the various organizations concerned with conservation in the context of the wider economic and planning systems within which they operate, and which to a large extent pre-condition their success or failure.

THE COUNTRY HOUSE AS A MICROCOSM

In the Autumn of last year there was an exhibition at the Victoria and Albert Museum: *The Destruction of the Country House*. It resulted from a study by John Cornforth,[8] which, although specifically related to the country house, presents in microcosm nearly all the points which are of prime relevance to conservation. The term 'Country House' helps to illuminate some of the psychology of the current conservation movement. It appears to stem from a reaction against the so-called pace of modern life, and the commercial architecture of post-war years, particularly its scale and materials,[9] and from the general economic and social uncertainty of the future. This has led many people, and certainly those active in civic societies, to an extensive interest not only in our social history as expressed in our buildings and pattern of settlements, but also in planning as practised and likely to change the established order; and to the belief that what is there today is likely to be better than what is there tomorrow, especially if it reflects a way of life in the spirit (if not exactly as practised) of the 'country house tradition'.

Defining What Should Be Conserved

Cornforth states that: 'Anyone interested has a fairly clear picture of a Country House but ... the Country House defies neat classification.' The problem of lack of definitional guidance does not arise for the generality of buildings and structures. The Department of the Environment defines ancient monuments, listed buildings and provides guidance for local authorities in designating conservation areas. This can be supplemented by the Council for British Archaeology's national assessment of historic towns. The great majority of ancient monuments are archaeological sites, ruins, or structures for which there is no present day use. The Secretary of State for the Environment has a duty to schedule buildings or structures above or below ground whose preservation is of national importance because of their historic, architectural, traditional, artistic or archaeological interest. Occupied dwelling houses and buildings in ecclesiastical use cannot be scheduled. The majority of listed buildings are occupied but there is an area of overlap—for example, barns, guildhalls and industrial structures.

The Investigators from the DOE have surveyed the whole country once, since the institution of listing in 1944, for buildings of 'special architectural or historic interest'. A resurvey is in progress, but is not expected to be complete for at least a further fifteen years. Principles of selection largely depend on the date of construction of the building.[10] Included in the list are all buildings built before 1700 which survive in anything like their original condition; most Georgian buildings (1700–1840); those between 1840 and 1914 of definite quality and character; exceptional buildings built after 1914. Buildings erected after 1939 are not eligible.

The Statutory List classifies these buildings according to their relative import-ance, into: Grade I, of outstanding interest, and Grade II, of special interest, of which particularly important buildings are given an asterisked marking. Many of those which used to be on a supplementary list, classified Grade III, are now being upgraded to the Statutory List; whilst those thought to be of local interest are included in a separate non-statutory list. Earl points out that, although:

'It is fairly easy to find petty faults, inconsistencies and omissions . . . the surprising thing is not that this great inventory is imperfect but that its standard of accuracy is so high . . . it is worth reflecting on the fact that its 250 000 entries have more often withstood detailed criticism than yielded to it.'[11]

The lists are in the course of revision, with about 25 000 new buildings (an average annual increase of about 20 per cent) having been added to the Statutory List each year between 1970 and 1973. This indicates the widening of views as to what is of architectural and historic interest as does the recommendation of the DOE[12] as to which buildings should be upgraded to the Statutory List, including those previously thought to be of modest quality, those which although now altered or refaced show some traces of ancient origin, and informal groups of mixed quality. Changes in taste, as well as compensation for earlier losses, are reflected in the fact that the terminal date for listing has been continually advanced to include Victorian and Edwardian buildings and examples of the Modern Movement.

Since the 1967 Civic Amenities Act, the concept of protection has been further extended from individual buildings to areas of special architectural and historic interest, thus recognizing the importance of setting and group value. Planning authorities are required to designate such areas with the object of preserving and enhancing their character and appearance.[13] Conservation areas can be classified as 'outstanding' by the Historic Buildings Council for the purposes of grant aid. Worskett points out:

'A major weakness lies in the varying standards of designation. Designation has been rampant in some areas (particularly it seems where there was a threat of a third London Airport) but in one or two counties has been non-existent. While the DOE and the Civic Trust gave a considerable amount of advice on how and what to designate, standards seem to vary in direct proportion to the personalities of [county] planning officers and their staff!'[14] (my brackets).

The Stock

'Trite as it may appear, not the least part of the problem is knowing its scale . . . no one knows how many notable country houses there are in England, Wales and Scotland.'

Cornforth's opinion, however, puts the figure at around 1 500 in England in 1972, and, on the assumption that they are all listed, they thus represent less than one per cent of all listed buildings in England at that date, of which there were about 160 000. At the end of 1974 the number of listed buildings in Great

Britain was just under 235 000. Only a small proportion are Grade I—when listing was completed for the first time in 1969–70 only about four per cent of all buildings on the Statutory List were of this grade.

Of conservation areas there were 3 165 in Great Britain in June 1974, of which 155 (five per cent) were considered to be outstanding (Table I); and of ancient monuments something of the order of 7–9 000 in England alone as at the end of 1971.[15] All of these lists are in the course of being added to.

A rought estimate of the total number of listed buildings in Great Britain when the present round of listing is completed is between 400 000 and 500 000. There are probably still a substantial number of conservation areas still to be designated. Of the 2 766 in England, 268 are in Greater London. Of the 2 500 remaining, 200 are in metropolitan counties and 550 in the Council for British Archaeology's recent list of 350 towns (see below). This leaves about 1 750 in the villages of England, which can be compared with the figure of 10 000 English Civil Parishes to obtain a very rough idea of the possible extent of further designation.

Obviously, there is substantial overlap between listed buildings and conservation areas; whilst we know the number of listed buildings we have no idea of the number of 'conserved buildings', that is, including those in conservation areas.

SIGNIFICANCE

We have very little idea of the significance of these buildings in numerical terms as part of our total stock of buildings, since there are no up-to-date figures available for the total numbers of buildings in the country (but, as a very rough guide, listed buildings in England and Wales as at 1974 represented just over one per cent of all rateable hereditaments). Such figures do not represent the significance of these buildings in terms either of their impact on the townscape and landscape or their 'value' to the community. For instance, country houses may have a much greater significance than one per cent of listed buildings because of their very 'scarceness' and because they are likely to have played a dominant part in their areas both architecturally and economically/socially due to the position in the community of the families which inhabited them. Visually, they may still be important. Even though their rôle may be changing, they may still be important economically and socially as, for instance, where they are converted to institutional use, or offices, or opened to the public, or used for community centres. Similar arguments can be applied to other 'conserved buildings'.

What is clear is that it is extremely difficult, if not virtually impossible, to value the significance of the buildings under discussion individually or collectively in money terms, which approach has anyway fallen into disrepute since the research team of the Roskill Commission valued Stewkley Church at its replacement cost. This represents a major problem for conservation, not because it should have a money value put on it, but because of the current tendency of planning to have insufficient regard for things which cannot be quantified. When faced with the decision whether to go for a more expensive location for a road, sewerage works, reservoir or other similar development which would, however, allow for 'conserved buildings' to be retained, in many instances our decision makers find great difficulty in opting for the more expensive alternative unless the intangible case for conservation can be put convincingly.

DISTRIBUTION

The distribution of this stock of buildings is of more significance than its total amount when considered from the point of view of accessibility to both residents and to tourists and visitors. Distribution is also important as a guide to where it may be necessary to direct financial or other forms of assistance, for instance, to areas of relatively low average income which may not be able to afford the costs of upkeep or to areas of major population and/or economic change where there may be pressure for redevelopment. Data is available on an area basis and can be analyzed, as for instance in Table 1 for Conservation Areas as designated in June 1974.

Obviously, this rough analysis (which needs to await completion of designations) could be greatly refined, for instance, to differentiate between conservation areas of various types and significance for their accessibility to residents and tourists, for the relative affluence of the various regions and so on. For example, from the figures in the table, the South-East and East Anglia would appear to provide the greatest 'conservation benefit' with the greatest number of conservation areas per 1 000 population; but, conversely, they have lower 'support populations' for each conservation area which may, or may not be, of concern

TABLE 1 *Conservation areas by standard region, June 1974*

Region	Numbers per Region	Percentage	(1971) Population per Conservation Area (Thousands)	Number Designated as Outstanding
South East	946	31	10.5	32
South West	316	10	12.1	35
London	268	9	27.6	21
West Midlands	254	8	20.4	21
Scotland	247	8	21.1	—
North West	214	7	31.3	15
East Anglia	184	6	9.2	12
East Midlands	170	6	20.0	5
North	161	5	20.5	10
Yorkshire and Humberside	154	5	31.2	4
Wales	152	5	17.8	—
Total:	3 165	100	17.6	155

Sources: Civic Trust Newsletter, July 1974/44.
Civic Trust Index of Conservation Areas, September 1971.
Census of Population 1971.

depending on the need for upkeep and the degree of affluence of the people in these areas.

OWNERSHIP AND USE

Out of a list of 950 country houses, Cornforth found that about 225 (24 per cent) had been adapted to other uses. About 582 (61 per cent) were still privately owned and 135 (14 per cent) belonged to the DOE, local authorities or the National Trust or the National Trust for Scotland; and about 36 per cent of those privately owned were open to the public, as were most of those belonging to the DOE/authorities/National Trusts.

No similar figures are available at a national, county or local level, for 'conserved buildings'. In other words, although it is generally assumed that the majority of the stock is dependent on private owners for its upkeep, the precise extent is not known, nor the extent to which they similarly depend on domestic use or commercial and other uses of various kinds.

DEMOLITIONS

In the last hundred years, Cornforth estimates that about 1 100 country houses have been wholly or partially demolished in Great Britain, of which 340 (30 per cent) have gone in the last 30 years. Apparently, there are threats on a similar scale to our heritage of landscape parks.[16] As regards losses of listed buildings, Insall comments that: 'In 1965, buildings on the Statutory List were being swept away at the rate of 400 or 500 each year ...'[17] These figures do not include those on the Supplementary List. Since 1970 the numbers totally or partially demolished per annum are still averaging about 400, but these are heavily offset by the increases in the total numbers of listed buildings (presumably due to upgrading from the Supplementary List), of which many probably come from those being added to the list, particularly as the need for 'spot listing' of threatened buildings is currently about 5 000 a year in England alone.

The Council for British Archaeology published a report in 1972 on the results of a special study of towns in England, Wales and Scotland of archaeological interest affected by modern development,[18] and concluded:

'Out of 906 historic towns, 834 remain which can be investigated. Of these, over half are threatened by some sort of development. 159 will be lost to archaeology in twenty years, if not before, including the most important towns of all historical periods. The archaeology of another 352 towns will in the next ten years be slowly, although not completely, eroded. The total of threatened towns is 511 excluding those already developed. The archaeology of only 21, and the architecture of only 11, of these towns is being adequately studied.'

The Rôle of the Private Owner

A number of factors affect the private owners' decisions as to use and upkeep. Cornforth demonstrates how the original role of the country house as a home for a wealthy family and employment centre for the locality has changed since the First World War in line with social and economic changes. These houses can be described as economically obsolete in terms of their original use in that the returns from the buildings are insufficient to cover the costs invested in them or provide an inadequate return as compared with other investments. In some cases, the value of the site for some other or more intensive use will be greater than the value of the building as a going concern.

Apart from the intangible return, valued by some people, which comes from occupying a 'conserved' building, the owner of any such building will be making his decisions on occupation, use and upkeep on financial grounds. He will consider the alternative ways in which he can use the building both in its current use and in other uses. Some of these will require greater capital investment than others, for instance in conversion as well as restoration, but may produce greater returns in rent or when sold. The alternatives may produce different 'lives' for the building in terms of the period it will last before requiring further major restoration (this period varies from 30–60 years or more depending on the building) or cease to be required for its current or converted use. Over the 'life' of the project for each alternative he will compare the streams of:

1. cost (capital costs of purchase, construction and subsequent reconstruction, fees and finance); and
2. revenue, either annual rents less annual maintenance and running costs, or capital value (the market capitalization of the net annual rents).

Other things being equal, he will make his decision on which alternative provides him with the greater return. Only if he can obtain a return sufficient to compensate him for his effort and expertise and at least as good as the return from investing his money elsewhere (allowing for differences in risk) will he use or restore the building. In this situation the owner, or potential owner, of a 'conserved' building is in the same situation as any other owner, and subject to the same considerations, except that he may not redevelop.

In some cases, he may obtain a greater return in the short term by carrying out the minimum of maintenance and letting it up as relatively cheap accommodation. This may be particularly so where there is a strong demand for such accommodation in areas where it is being gradually eroded by new development and is often the case in or on the fringe of a central area where listed buildings are often also located. For instance, this is true behind Carnaby Street in Westminster, where there is a demand for workrooms from the 'rag' trade and relatively cheap small shops and office suites.[19]

This kind of calculation is now familiar in the field of rehabilitation of housing[20] and here it is sometimes surprising how much it is worth spending on rehabilitation of even some of the most decayed buildings before redevelopment becomes a better proposition.[21] Although very little collated data is available on which to base conclusions, the reverse is often true for 'conserved buildings', particularly those needing materials which are now relatively expensive such as Bath Stone, lead guttering, or where all that is retained of the building is its shell, as for instance the Nash Terraces around Regent's Park. Where conversion to offices is envisaged, costs are often similar per unit to redevelopment (particularly where air conditioning is inserted) and the amount of lettable office floorspace often less.

In some cases the costs of maintenance far outweigh the costs of rent to the occupier and these, together with rates, may be of more importance than rent in his consideration of whether he will continue to use the building.[22] Cornforth points out the sharp increase in repair costs for historic buildings which have risen by an average of between 55 per cent and 60 per cent in the two years between March 1972 and March 1974 and even 100 per cent in some cases, as compared with the official figure of a 48 per cent increase for new building in that period. Labour costs are invariably proportionately higher in restoration than in new work and, because of the need for special skills and the high cost of training it is likely that the cost of restoration will continue to go up faster than that of new work.

Capital or rental value will depend primarily on the following factors:

1. the amount, quality and kind of accommodation provided by the building and its location;
2. the quality of the surrounding environment;
3. the amount and quality of 'competing' property;
4. the income of potential purchasers and occupiers which in turn depend on the general level of economic activity in the area;
5. the availability of finance to potential purchasers and occupiers which depends on the view taken taken by the investing institution, bank or other finance source of the quality of the building and enterprise as an investment;
6. legislation.

Most of these factors are, or can be, influenced by the community via planning and financial controls and arrangements as part of the planning system.

Many 'conserved buildings' tend to lend themselves to use or conversion for small organizations. For example, they can be converted into a number of flats distinguishable from each other because of a different arrangement and size of rooms or ceiling heights; or small suites of offices one to each floor; or small specialist shops. Particularly where shops and some types of office are concerned, these are the kind of organizations which in some cases, whilst they may initially be able to afford the rents and cost of maintenance, do not always represent good covenants in terms of security to the owner due to the riskiness of the business and lack of financial reserves. The speed of turnover in occupiers in the King's Road, Chelsea is an example. This higher risk is discounted at a higher rate in the market, giving a lower capital value to the completed investment as compared with more modern buildings and where larger organizations are tenants. This is probably the reason, coupled with greater difficulty of management, why the majority of commercial developers have not shown a great deal of interest in 'conserved buildings'. However, there are signs that the market's view may be changing particularly for offices, where in today's circumstances it may be wise to spread the risk amongst a number of tenants rather than rely on the financial stability of only one.

Rates were mentioned above, but taxes of other kinds, particularly the proposed capital transfer and wealth taxes, are also important factors for country houses, although their possible effect on other 'conserved' buildings is not yet clear.

Those which could be particularly vulnerable are the historic town houses, the smaller historic country houses and those 'conserved buildings' occupied by small businesses.

The Rôle of Public and Private Organizations

Where buildings become obsolete for one reason or another they are adapted and eventually abandoned or redeveloped by their owners. If the community places a social value of some kind on the building for instance, because of its architectural, historic or group interest, then there is a need for the Government or some other organization to intervene in the market process to ensure its retention in a reasonable condition and preferably to serve a useful purpose. If possible, the building should be so restored or converted that it becomes economically self-conserving—where the financial returns from the building are sufficient to attract, and go on attracting, the investment required to retain and run it.

Such intervention, as practised in this century, began with the Ancient Monuments Act of 1913 and increased through a series of Acts of which the most recent is the Town and Country Amenities Act 1974. Within the government framework there are advisory bodies: the Ancient Monuments Boards for England, Wales and Scotland and the Historic Buildings Councils for England, Wales and Scotland. Government provides protection, finance and advice. It can acquire buildings, provide grants and can enhance and influence the economic, social and physical environment for conservation via its planning function. This latter role is discussed in the section on conservation as part of the economic and planning system.

There is a large number of private organizations in the country providing advice, interest and finance in this field. Among the most prominent societies administering trust funds are the National Trust, the Pilgrim Trust, the Mutual Households Association Limited, the Incorporated Church Building Society, the Historic Churches Preservation Trust and the National Association of Almshouses.

PROTECTION

In recent years protective legislation has increased. Alteration or demolition of a listed building requires Listed Building Consent in addition to the normal planning permission from the local authority. Local authorites can issue repairs notices. Unlisted buildings in conservation areas require local authority consent for demolition. Trees in such areas are given added protection. Listed Churches, although often important in group value, are not protected. After a monument has been scheduled, three months notice must be given to the DOE of any proposed alteration. To protect threatened buildings which have not yet been listed and ancient monuments, local authorities have power to serve emergency Building Preservation Notices which remain in force for six months to give time for listing. There are expropriation and substantial fine/imprisonment provisions.

The legislation is generally now regarded as effective for listed buildings and the number illegally demolished or altered is very small. Control of demolition of unlisted buildings in conservation areas was only introduced last year as a result of much controversy over the destruction of the physical and social 'setting' of listed buildings in these areas, particularly in Bath. However, legislation can only encourage action and works as a final sanction. Its effectiveness depends on active and enlightened administration, particularly at county and district level. Whilst the powers are available, the difficulty is in involving the financial commitment of public and private funds.

FINANCE

Central government grants are made available through the Historic Buildings Councils. Between them they cover repairs to the structure and contents of buildings, for the upkeep of grounds and environmental improvement. They are given to outstanding buildings (since 1953), to outstanding groups of buildings (since 1955), outstanding conservation areas (since 1972). Heritage Year grants are specifically for 1975 and are for ancillary improvements in non-outstanding conservation areas. In 1953 the Government was prepared to provide funds of £250 000 per annum; this was increased to £450 000 in 1964, and £1 000 000 in 1971. Since 1953, a total of over £12 million has been offered in grants.[23] There is no separate system set up for classifying buildings for grant purposes. The principles of selection emerge from the applications received. Similarly there is no system for deciding priorities as between areas according, perhaps, to need or in line with a national policy for tourism.

In addition, the National Land Fund was set up in the Finance Act of 1946 with a capital of £50 million, reduced to £10 million in 1957. Its function is to reimburse the Inland Revenue for historic houses, gardens, amenity lands and chattels accepted by the State in lieu of estate duties and to reimburse the Secretary of State for purchase under the 1953 Historic Buildings and Ancient Monuments Act when no other means can be found to preserve a threatened building of the very first importance. Its functions may become more important in the future with the proposed fiscal changes.

The Historic Buildings Councils and local government combine together in the system of Town Schemes where they jointly meet 50 per cent[24] of the cost of structural repairs in outstanding areas for buildings which do not individually qualify for a national or local grant. The number of places operating town schemes has risen from 25 in 1970/71 to 60 in 1974/75. The Government's total allocation of funds for town schemes is about £400 000 in the current year. House improvement grants are another form of central/local government partnership which can be applied to 'conserved buildings'. Figures do not exist for the numbers of such buildings which have been assisted in this way, but figures for Warwick and Lincoln[23] show the significance of this source for those towns. For instance, in Warwick, with more than 350 listed buildings, improvement grants of £42 000 have been made in respect of 28 per cent of them.

The Redundant Churches Fund is a similar partnership between the Church of England and the Secretary of State; it was established in 1969 for the conservation of churches of architectural and historic interest with a sum of £500 000 set aside for the period 1st April 1969 to 31st December 1974.

In addition to this system local authorities have powers under the Local Authorities (Historic Buildings) Act 1962 to make discretionary grants and loans for the repair and maintenance of the fabric of listed buildings, including churches of all denominations. It appears that many authorities are reluctant to use these powers, but expenditure has increased from a figure of £13 500 in 1962 to £344 000 in 1971/72. A recent survey by the Civic Trust of about 40 per cent of all local authorities in England and Scotland showed that only 27 per cent of those responding had made grants and/or loans for historic buildings over the period 1970/73.[23]

The amount of money spent by private organizations varies. The total expenditure of the National Trust on buildings, coast and countryside, has risen from £1.831 million in 1964 to £5.697 million in 1973. Total grants authorized by the Pilgrim Trust for building preservation in 1971 were £343 000. Since its inception in 1952, the Historic Churches Preservation Trust had given grants to the value of about £1.5 million. In addition, much work in rescuing and adapting buildings for modern use has been done by local trusts. The Civic Trust made a survey of their work[25] which recommended the establishment of a National Building Conservation Fund to help them. The report stated:

'It is not possible to estimate with anything approaching precision the amount of new money required to make an appreciable impact on the restoration of listed buildings. There is no firm evidence as to the number of buildings at risk, or where they are, or what their state of repair may be. On the basis of a series of indicators this report suggests no more than that £3 million, employed through local revolving funds, could bring about a noticeable expansion of preservation activity. In practice this amount might be found to be insufficient.'

Some of these trusts retain their buildings and rely on income to build up sufficient funds to continue the work on other buildings. Others operate on a revolving fund principle whereby the completed buildings are sold, thus speeding up the obtaining of sufficient finance and the number of restorations carried out.

Whereas data is available on many other forms of public and private expenditure, it is extremely difficult to sort out global figures for expenditure on 'conserved buildings and areas'. A rough estimate of current expenditure per annum in Great Britain for 1974 and 1975 for central and local government and those private organizations mentioned above, except the National Trusts, would be in the region of £3.0/£3.5 million (excluding that associated with housing rehabilitation). These figures exclude expenditure by private individuals (except where matching town schemes), for which there is no information.

How far has investment kept pace with need? Expenditure on a similar basis to that above was probably running at about £0.75 million in 1963. Table 2 shows some comparative figures from which conservation would appear to be doing rather well in terms of the percentage change between 1963 and 1973,

TABLE 2   *Comparative increases*

Item £m	1973 Expenditure (1970 prices)	Percentage Change 1963/73*
1. Conserved Buildings	2.17/2.53	+201/+234
2. G.D.P.	56 132	+134
3. Consumers' Expenditure	35 759	+130
4. Public Authorities' Expenditure	10 109	+126
5. ,, on housing	1 228	+166
6. Building Costs Index		+199

Sources: 1. Estimate as above.
          2, 3, 4. Annual Abstract of Statistics 1974.
          5. Lloyd's Bank.
          6. Spons Builders Price Book 1975.
          * Estimates on a constant price basis for each item.

but rather badly in terms of the absolute amount of expenditure; for instance, expenditure on conservation is less than 0.2 per cent of public authorities' expenditure on housing.

ADVICE

There is a number of public and private organizations concerned with finding new uses for buildings and advising on methods of restoration. For instance, there is the Historic Buildings Bureau, which is part of the DOE, where owners who wish to buy or sell historic buildings may register with the Bureau, which distributes a list (containing usually 60 or so buildings) to possible purchasers and provides professional advice on possible alternative uses. A similar service is provided by the Society for the Protection of Ancient Buildings, and the Georgian Society. The DOE has published two booklets describing schemes as examples of what can be done.[26]

The Civic Trust is an independent body formed to support and advise local civic societies. The Council for Small Industries in Rural Areas exists to co-ordinate and encourage local craftsmen and maintain traditional crafts, but as Cornforth states:

'There is a very real shortage of architects with the right degree of sympathy for restoration work and adequate training and experience. Efforts are being made to develop training programmes that carry a professional qualification, but, as yet, apart from the course at the University of York, nothing has been established. And although there are signs of a new interest in craftsmanship, this has not yet been harnessed to adequate training programmes or to a proper career structure . . . it will take a long time to solve these problems, but it would be easier to make plans if more was known about the future pattern of potential restoration work.'

Some Familiar Dilemmas

However, despite the legislation, finance, advice and large number of organizations which have evolved in the last thirty years or so to tackle the problems of conservation, conservationists still face a number of dilemmas. These dilemmas tend to polarize around the set of problems associated with 'underuse' and the need to intensify or find new uses to provide sufficient income to prevent 'conserved buildings' falling into decay; and the other set of problems associated with 'overuse' and the need to resist pressure for redevelopment.

Economic growth is often cited as the prime enemy particularly associated with the problems of 'overuse'. As the economy and social life of a town expands and changes, there comes a point at which redevelopment of its obsolete parts becomes necessary if it is to keep pace with current requirements. This occurs particularly in city centres where, in most cases, the majority of buildings of architectural and historic interest are likely to be located. Should the size of settlement, therefore, be restructured in the interests of conservation? Should the traditional town centre always be the location for expansion and improvement of shops, offices, entertainment, civic offices or would suburban or out-of-town locations be more desirable? Proposals for out-of-town shopping centres, for example, often bring forth cries of alarm from shopkeepers and landowners about the effects of loss of trade with warnings of future disuse and decay. But there may equally well be occasions when relief of commercial pressure may be of greater benefit, especially where the cost and disruption arising from new roads required to serve the expanding centre are taken into account.[27]

Similarly, associated with the growth both of population and in the economy are the conservation problems arising from expansion of movement and the need to improve the transport system where new roads in towns may be inappropriate in scale; and where ease of commuting may bring pressure for expansion of villages to such a degree that, whilst the building may be conserved, the original village pattern may be destroyed not only for individual villages but also for a pattern of settlements across an area of countryside.

However, where there are conservation problems associated with 'underuse', growth of the economy is likely to be as much an ally as an enemy, providing a demand for buildings and their consequent upkeep if they can be adapted to modern requirements. Thus it may be appropriate to encourage economic and population growth in towns where there is a shortfall of this kind. For example, it has been suggested (in jest) that one of the ways of finding purchasers for residential buildings in the walled city of York would be to move the Norwich Union up there! Similarly, conservation considerations could figure in deciding priorities for regional transport improvements with a view to influencing demand for employment and retailing in ways which could either assist or hinder conservation of the fabric.

A further aspect of economic growth is that there is a good deal of evidence that an interest in conservation is something which comes from an education and from a fairly comfortable standard of living backed up by the income necessary to indulge it—so much so that conservationists are considered by some to be an elitist group.[28] This raises the further dilemma of the desirability or otherwise of the 'gentrification' of conserved residential areas which, incidentally, do not necessarily produce a corresponding demand in conserved shopping areas for the traditional grocers, bakers who originally occupied them, but for shops of other kinds such as boutiques, antiques. As a result of these social changes the buildings may be retained, but the original social atmosphere and purpose of the area lost. The country house is an illustration, having (for an increasing number of houses) changed its rôle from a family home to one of recreation for the general public.

Conservation as Part of the Economic and Planning System

These dilemmas are properly within the scope of central and local government as part of regional and county strategic economic and planning policy. However, the tendency has been in the main, to deal with conservation on an individual building or group of buildings restoration basis, rather than by trying at the same time to influence the underlying economic forces. It needs to be seen as part of an integrated and comprehensive management system for the urban environment where all the components (housing, central area, employment, transportation ...) are appreciated as part of the same system rather than as separate bits, as is still the unfortunate tendency of planning[29] despite recent thinking to the contrary.[30]

A policy of conservation, once the buildings have been adapted internally as far as possible, imposes a constraint on the capacity of an area to adapt to changing economic and social circumstances. What are the economic and social consequences of such a policy of 'minimum physical change'? Figure 1 is an attempt to highlight some of the complexity of the economic and social life of a city as it finally affects the use and value of individual properties and consequently the decisions of owners (both private and public) as to upkeep. Four possible effects of such a policy are suggested and the points where they could affect the system indicated. What happens, for instance to the industries and services which make up the city's economic base by earning money from outside if they are not provided with space to expand, or faced with a smaller supply of labour (because houses are not provided for an expanding labour force), or greater transport costs because of congestion, or in the case of tourism, provided with a more attractive asset in a wholly conserved city? As a consequence, what happens to the industries and services which serve them, to the income levels of the citizens and consequently to their demands for shops, entertainment, social services—all activities which make up the varied life and prosperity of the place? What happens to the value of property of different kinds and the ability of the city to attract investment to maintain itself? How much may be needed from central government conservation grants? And if it is possible to understand and predict what will happen to this complex system, are the consequences better or worse in terms of the needs and priorities of the citizens as compared with what would otherwise have taken place under more conventional policies? Such a study is

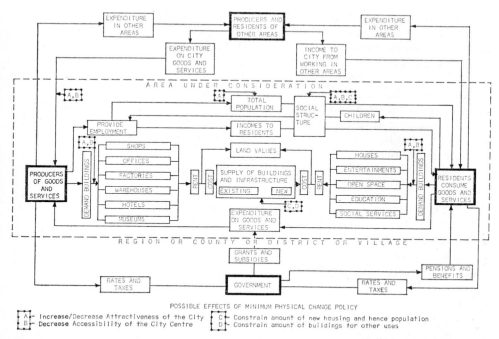

Fig. 1   A stylized city system, highlighting the complexity of the economic and social life of a city

about to be undertaken for Bath,[31] a city which appears to have potentially many of the problems associated with 'overuse'.

A similar approach would apply to areas experiencing the problems of 'underuse'. For example, setting aside the question of through traffic which it has in common with Bath, would increasing the accessibility of the centre of York by building the inner ring road or improving public transport solve some of the problems of 'underuse' of upper floors and backland areas in the walled city? Would a greater effect in this respect be achieved by encouraging firms or other organizations (York already has a university) to locate there and expand, thereby altering the employment structure and attracting occupiers for the kind of buildings available? In towns such as York tourism is often seen as the saving grace, whilst in others worries are expressed about there being too many tourists overwhelming what they have come to see: for example, San Marco in August.[32]

In all cases, the problem is one of establishing the capacity of the area for change and of the 'right' balance between conservation and redevelopment.

STRATEGIC

It will be apparent that the problems of towns such as Bath and York, or even of a pattern of settlements such as those in parts of East Anglia, cannot be dealt with in isolation; there may be a need to siphon off pressure for growth, as in the case of Bath, or encourage it, as in the case of York. These matters will need to be dealt with in the County Structure Plan. Essential steps would be:

c

1. To establish the pattern of conservation throughout the county both in the villages and towns and their problems (if any) of under or over use;
2. To establish the capacity of these areas for further change both for the buildings and infrastructure (particularly transportation);
3. In line with concurrent studies of population, employment, transport, retailing . . . to establish the underlying reasons for the problems and possible methods of tackling them. At the strategic level these methods will relate primarily to the deployment of future changes in population, employment and transportation. The aim would be to match capacity with demand as far as possible;
4. To consider the weight to be given to the resulting set of conservation policies and their implications in the generation and evaluation of alternatives for the Structure Plan as a whole.

A more empirical approach to conservation than is usual in such plans was made in the studies for the Strategic Plan for the South East, and the problems resulting from rapid population growth were identified.[33] Advice on similar lines is being provided by the Historic Areas Conservation Division of the DOE to other Regional Strategy Teams.

LOCAL

Obviously at the strategic level the relative priority of conservation and the scope for having an effect on individual areas and buildings will be less than at the local plan level, where more detailed considerations can be applied. Here, the need to establish the problems in more detail and the characteristics of the stock in relation to these problems (extent, significance, distribution, ownership, use) will be important, particularly where there are multiple ownerships.[34] Where there are limited resources available to spend on conservation, it may be necessary to establish a system of priorities for investment related to need and importance, leading to a rolling programme of investment.[35,36] The aim would be to make the buildings economically self-supporting as far as possible by enhancing their capital or rental values to a level sufficient to justify the costs involved and/or to minimize the amount of grant needed. This does not always necessarily mean subsequent occupation by the 'highest bidder', for instance, where this use would be incompatible with the character of the building or area as the garden centre/builders merchants may be in the restored Richmond Station; or where the buildings could be used for some 'social' use.[37]

As pointed out above, most of the factors on which values depend can be influenced by planning. For instance, it is possible to influence the level and pattern of commercial values in a town centre by controlling the amount and location of new commercial development, and particularly for shops, the location of the generators (bus stations, car parks) and attractors (variety stores, specialist shops) of shoppers.[38,39] New shops inserted behind conserved buildings, of which some examples are those in the cities of Chester, Salisbury and Colchester, may have the effect of creating a demand for the conserved buildings to be used as shops or, where too much new shopping is inserted, conversely draw trade away. Similarly, the amount of 'competing' property, the surrounding environment, levels of economic activity are all factors which can be influenced both in their overall levels and precise locations. At this level, such policies thus require detailed knowledge of the economic and financial as well as the visual factors (which are those usually studied) affecting conservation.

Conclusion

There is a great deal of activity concerned with conservation, both in government and among the public. At the present time much of this is directed towards its architectural and historical and, sometimes, social, characteristics rather than those that are economic and financial, and it is rarely seen in its proper relationship to the wider economic and planning systems. However, it is within these latter aspects where lie the clues to the tackling of the dilemmas which still remain. In many ways, it can be argued that conservation is that area of planning where quantification has the least part to play. Nevertheless, some analysis and quantification must be attempted if our limited resources for conservation are to be spent most effectively and for conservation to find its proper level amongst competing objectives.

NOTES AND REFERENCES

1 Summerson, J., *Heavenly Mansions*, London, Cresset Press, 1947.

2 Where opposition has been concerned with the use of the buildings as well as the fabric. 150 small businesses pay rents of about £2.50 per square foot. Rents in the new building may be about £15.00 per square foot and the existing businesses would find it very difficult to get similar accommodation in central London where the stock of small and cheap office space is dwindling. *Architects' Journal*, Vol. 160, Nos. 41 and 42 (October 1974).

3 Dick, Andrew H. S., 'Finance for Conservation', *The Planner*, Vol. 60, No. 10, (December 1974), pp. 948–952.

4 Dobby, Alan, 'Conservation and Planning', *The Planner*, Vol. 61, No. 1, (January 1975), pp. 11–13.

5 Coddington, Alan, 'The Economics of Conservation' in Warren, A. and Goldsmith, F. B. (Eds.), *Conservation in Practice*, London, Wiley, 1974, pp. 453–464.

6 Lichfield, Nathaniel and Associates, 'Economics of Conservation' in Esher, Viscount (Ed.), *York: A Study in Conservation*, London, HMSO, 1968, Appendix 6, pp. 239–248.

7 Kennet, Wayland, 'The Politics of Conservation' in Warren, A. and Goldsmith, F. B., op. cit., pp. 465–475.

8 Cornforth, John, *Country Houses in Britain: Can they Survive?*, London, Country Life, 1974.

9 See, for instance, MacEwen, Malcolm, 'The Folly of Modern Architecture', *Illustrated London News*, December 1974, pp. 51–53.

10 Department of the Environment, *Circular 102/74: Town and Country Planning Act 1971, Historic Buildings and Conservation*, London, HMSO, 1974.

11 Earl, John, 'Listed Buildings and the Laws of Preservation', *Chartered Surveyor*, (February 1972), p. 398.

12 Department of the Environment, *Circular 102/74*, op. cit.

13 Department of the Environment, *Circular 53/67: Civic Amenities Act 1967, Parts I and II*, London, HMSO, 1967.

14 Worksett, Roy, 'Great Britain: Progress in Conservation', *Architectural Review*, Vol. CLVII, No. 935, (January 1975), pp. 9–18.

15 Department of the Environment, *List of Ancient Monuments in England, Corrected to 31st*

December 1971, London, HMSO, 1973. Department of the Environment, Scottish Development Department.

16 Binney, M. and Burman, P., 'Assault by Motorway, Landscape Parks in Danger', *Country Life*, August 15 1974, pp. 418–420.

17 Insall, Donald, *The Case of Old Buildings Today*, London, Architectural Press, 1972, p. 13.

18 Council for British Archaeology, *The Erosion of History: Archaeology and Planning in Towns*, London, Council for British Archaeology, 1972, p. 30.

19 Lichfield, Nathaniel and Associates, *Newburgh Street, Financial Comparison of Alternatives*. unpublished, 1974.

20 See, for instance, Needleman, L., 'The Comparative Economics of Improvement and New Buildings', *Urban Studies*, Vol. 6, No. 2, (June 1969), pp. 196–209.

21 Lichfield, Nathaniel and Associates, *Gurney Valley Villages Study, Part II: Technical Appendix No. 3, Details of Financial Appraisal*, London, 1971.

22 Lichfield, Nathaniel and Associates, *Richmond Town Centre Survey: Survey of Shopkeepers' Costs Related to the Buildings*, unpublished, 1975.

23 Dick, Andrew H. S., op. cit.

24 In Bath and Whitehaven, 75 per cent grants are made.

25 Civic Trust, *Financing the Preservation of Old Buildings*, London, Civic Trust, 1971.

26 Department of the Environment, *New Life for Old Buildings*, London, HMSO, 1971; Department of the Environment, *New Life for Historic Areas*, London, HMSO, 1972.

27 See, for instance, the arguments relating to the future growth of Cambridge in Lewis, J. Parry, *A Study of the Cambridge Sub-Region*, London, HMSO, 1974.

28 Eversley, D., 'Conservation for the Minority', *Built Environment*, Vol. 3, No. 1, pp. 14–15.

29 For example, the continued separation of transportation from planning in most county departmental organizations within the framework of corporate planning.

30 To quote only one reference, Chadwick, G., *A Systems View of Planning*, Oxford, Pergamon Press, 1971.

31 Lichfield, Nathaniel and Associates, *Bath Steering Group Minimum Physical Change Study Project Report*, unpublished, 1975.

32 Dower, M., 'Tourism and Conservation', *Architects' Journal*, May 1974, pp. 941–985.

33 South East Joint Planning Team, *Strategic Plan for the South East; Studies, Volume 2: Social and Environmental Aspects*, London, HMSO, 1971, pp. 101–132.

34 For instance, the Dutch houses in Bridge Street, Chester as described in Worskett, Roy, op. cit., p. 18.

35 Lichfield, Nathaniel and Associates, *Colchester Town Centre Conservation Study, Suggested Approach*, unpublished, 1970.

36 Bath City Architect and Planning Officer, *Conservation Study and Programme: Terms of Reference and Staff Needs*, Bath, 1975.

37 Bugler, Jeremy, 'Is this What Heritage Year is all About?', *Observer Magazine*, 29 December 1974, pp. 20–23.

38 Leonard, Vincent, Gorbing, Raymond and Partners; Lichfield, Nathaniel and Associates, *Redevelopment in Colchester Central Area*, Colchester, 1970.

39 For a comprehensive view of retailing and conservation, see Whitbourn, P. R., *Retailing and the Conservation of Historic Centres*, unpublished Ph.D. Thesis, University College, London, 1973.

ACKNOWLEDGMENTS

I am most grateful for the research assistance of Jennifer McGrandle; to Michael Edwards for helpful advice on regional planning; and to Gerald Blundell and Michael Burroughs for sorting me out on the figures in Table 2.

Chester

Conservation in Practice

D. ANNE DENNIER

The City of Chester has gained a reputation as a leader among Britain's historic cities in conserving its heritage. In 1966 it was chosen as one of four towns in which the implications of conservation policies were studied under joint commissions from the government and the local authorities concerned. Following this study the City Council declared the whole of the historic centre a Conservation Area, some 200 acres (80 hectares) with 600 listed buildings. It has appointed a Conservation Officer with a small staff, including two Clerks of Works, whose principal task is to liaise between the local authority and owners, architects and contractors engaged in conservation work. A Conservation Fund was established in 1969, with a specific rate levy, and grants have been attracted from government funds. The sums have been increased so that £200 000 is available from public sources in the current financial year, most of which is allocated. Several conservation schemes were sufficiently far advanced to be completed by or during European Architectural Heritage Year, and Chester was chosen as one of four British Pilot Projects for 1975. Such a record undoubtedly points to very considerable achievements.

In this chapter I shall outline the development of the conservation programme and consider some of the problems of assessing its success, then I shall set conservation policy in the wider context of planning the city centre and examine some of the problems of planning the next stages of conservation and development.

The Background to the Conservation Programme

The consultants appointed to the 1966 study were Donald Insall and Associates. Their report,[1] published in 1968, outlined their approach which had been 'to study the city in depth whilst avoiding the temptation to reduce any complex living place to the terms of a sterile equation'. They defined their aims as 'to pioneer a method of conservation and to guide the future development of a particular city'. In their report they laid great stress on the importance of money and management in achieving results. They emphasized the need for confidence in the future stability and economic success of an area if it was to attract investment from public and private sources which would have to be financed over a period of some years. They underlined the importance of there being a 'specific policy and plan for a defined conservation area'. This, they said, included incentives to repair, and a programme of public expenditure on circulation and environmental improvements.

Important as the study was for Chester, it also had a national value, for as well as illustrating methods of approach and possible lines of attack on the problems of conservation, the consultants looked at legal and administrative problems. Many of their recommendations were taken up by the Preservation Policy Group in the Ministry of Housing and Local Government (which coordinated the findings of the four studies) and were incorporated in the Civic Amenities Act 1967 and subsequent Town and Country Planning Acts.

This legislation was but one manifestation of a growing national concern for the fabric of our historic cities. It has enabled local authorities to declare conservation areas, to tighten controls both over listed buildings and their immediate surroundings, and, of more consequence in the total urban scene, to use similar controls over demolition and alterations to other buildings in such an area. The declaration of a conservation area, though valuable as a statement of intent, means little until it becomes clear how much an authority is willing to back its intentions in hard cash. Equally the government's legislation has needed the backing of exchequer contributions to conservation. These have been forthcoming; more money than ever before is available from national sources both for the conservation of a wider range of old buildings and for environmental improvements in conservation areas.

But the key to successful conservation must lie in local action and commitment. In Chester the decisions taken in 1969 to declare the historic city a Conservation Area and to tackle the problems of financing work and of management set the current programme in motion.

The Conservation Programme

The rate levy for the Conservation Fund was set in 1970/71 at two pence with a yield of £29 200 a year. The idea proved sufficiently successful, and politically acceptable, for the levy to be increased to yield £55 275 in 1973/74 and £100 000 in 1974/75. The new District Council (still referred to as the City Council) took over responsibility for the City and two former Rural Districts in April 1974 and continues to maintain the fund at £100 000 per annum. The government agreed to a Town Scheme covering the Conservation Area in 1970/71 and allocated £10 000 that year. This contribution, too, has risen, and since 1973/74 the Department of the Environment has matched the City's expenditure up to a total of £100 000 a year. Grants under the Town Scheme are usually allocated on the basis of the owner financing 50 per cent of the work and the Department and the City each contributing 25 per cent. However, the situation is complicated by the fact that the City owns some of the most important property, Bishop Lloyd's House for example, which is also among the most difficult and expensive to restore or repair. Even willing owners sometimes find difficulty in raising loans on old property, and on occasion the City may have to step in to keep the scheme going as they did, for instance, in the case of the Dutch Houses, by buying some of the interests. Altogether, money now available from public funds represents a total annual investment of some £400 000.

The city took an unusual step in engaging staff with a particular responsibility in the management of the conservation programme. While the main task remains that of negotiating and monitoring applications grants, contracts and building work, much has been added to the job. The Conservation Office now provides a vital, and above all easily accessible, link in the chain of information. Anyone with a 'problem' building can find help and advice there. Local public interest and visitors' interest are catered for in the publications, posters and exhibitions which are organized and publicized with the help of the City's resuscitated Information Office and a sympathetic local press. A redundant city centre church, St. Michael's, was opened during June as the Chester Heritage Centre. A formidable programme of events on the EAHY theme, including Heritage Walks and day tours accompanied by the Consultant and the Conservation Officer, is being organized during the year.

A number of voluntary organizations are concerned with the future of the historic city and its buildings, including the Chester Civic Trust and the Council for the Protection of Rural England. These organizations are represented on the Conservation Area Advisory Committee which is able to comment on proposals and planning applications. This, of course, can be an awkward task where any group disagree with the majority or with the Council's eventual decision but the Committee performs a valuable function in discussing proposals and publicizing them especially among those groups most interested in, and committed to, maintaining the historic centre of the city. The degree of accord which apparently exists in Chester is worth remarking on; neither the conservation policies nor planning decisions have aroused the heated controversy or the organized opposition which has been seen in other historic cities such as Bath and York.

Continuity in management over a period of years can be an important factor in achieving confidence and consistency in planning and conservation policies. Fortunately, in Chester, local government reorganization has brought no noticeable changes in its wake. Many officers and members continue with the new authority; the same consultants have been retained; there have been no unexpected changes in policy and, while some competition for Conservation Fund resources for buildings outside the Conservation Area may yet develop, both the city centre projects and the Fund have been maintained.

The Conservation Programme in Practice

There have been three interlocking themes in realizing the conservation programme: restoration of important buildings, concerted action on the various problems caused by neglect in the Bridgegate Action Area, and the on-going control of new development so that it sits sympathetically with its neighbours.

Several rescue and restoration schemes on individual buildings have now been completed or are in progress. Very few buildings had been tackled before the programme got underway, although work had started on some, notably the 'nine houses'. This was a row of seventeenth century, half-timbered cottages which had become uninhabitable. They were bought by the City to prevent redevelopment of the site and then restored with the help of a government grant.

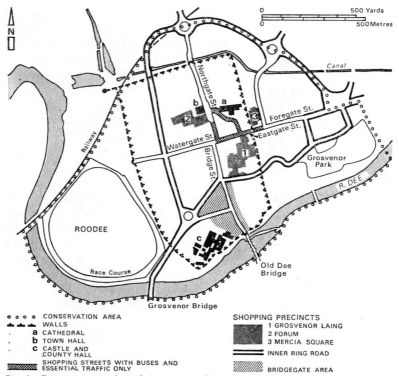

○ ○ ○ ○ CONSERVATION AREA
▲▲▲ WALLS
. a CATHEDRAL
. b TOWN HALL
. c CASTLE AND
    COUNTY HALL
SHOPPING STREETS WITH BUSES AND
ESSENTIAL TRAFFIC ONLY

SHOPPING PRECINCTS
1 GROSVENOR LAING
2 FORUM
3 MERCIA SQUARE
INNER RING ROAD
BRIDGEGATE AREA

Fig. 1   Diagrammatic plan of the centre of the City of Chester, showing the city walls, the inner ring road, new commercial developments and pedestrianization schemes. The location of the Bridgegate Action Area is also shown

Grant aid, since 1969, has naturally been concentrated on the more important buildings which are at greater risk through neglect and disrepair, some of which have, indeed, been in danger of collapsing. Not all the buildings listed in the Insall Report as being in urgent need of attention have yet been restored but those that have include: an early eighteenth century house, Shipgate House, at the bottom of Lower Bridge Street; in the same street, Tudor House, a curious mixture of Tudor and Georgian architecture, and Gamul House, a Jacobean hall; in Bridge Street, the Dutch Houses and a little half-timbered house, formerly St. Michael's Rectory, which has a particularly fine interior; and 51 Watergate Street which is the first phase of a scheme to restore Bishop Lloyd's House, an early seventeenth century house with an elaborately carved façade (Plates 3–5, 7).

The restoration of such properties has frequently involved very substantial reconstruction. For instance, a new side wall has been built at Tudor House, the roof of Gamul House has been completely rebuilt and a concealed reinforced concrete ring beam put in at eaves level, and, in the case of the Dutch Houses, a steel and concrete frame now supports the reconstructed façade. Meticulous attention has been paid to detail and some older features restored, such as an elliptical window lost from the top storey of Gamul House and the older pattern of fenestration used in the Dutch Houses.

Much of this work, in the end, is hidden from public view, in the structure or the interior of the building. Externally, with very few exceptions such as the rather flamboyant Dutch Houses, the key to successful conservation is understatement: the building does not stand out, it simply looks right. Thus the skilfully carved barge boards of St. Michael's Rectory, the pattern copied from an old drawing, are a feature more for the connoisseur than the passing shopper who may notice only that the building looks fresh and clean and that the woodwork is a lighter colour than usual. Much of Chester's charm lies in the huddle of vernacular and domestic architecture of several centuries and it is a measure of the visual success of the restoration schemes that they enhance this charm. It is perhaps, a little unfair that the comparatively simple process of cleaning big stone buildings such as the Town Hall, The Gates and St. Michael's Church has had a greater visual impact in the general scene. In this, the special Environmental Assistance Scheme has added its contribution to the improvement of the city's environment to the tune of 75 per cent grants towards the cost of cleaning the buildings over a two year period.

It can also be counted a success that uses have been found for the restored buildings. Some, St. Michael's Rectory and the Dutch Houses for example, continue as commercial premises. Gamul House is to be an exhibition room and meeting room which will be available to the public. Tudor House provides its owner with business premises and a home. The greatest obstacle to finding an economic use for restored buildings remains the problem of conversion. The upper floors of four- and five-storey buildings, especially on narrow frontages, have little commercial value and, as the consultants pointed out, lack of use leads to decay. The difficulties of overcoming fire hazards and access problems still inhibit conversion to residential use so that, even in the Dutch Houses which the City owns, the problems of converting the upper floors to flats had not been resolved at the time of writing.

The Bridgegate Area was noted in the Insall Report as one where action on several fronts was needed to dispel the blight of long standing neglect. It lies to the south of the city centre between the River and the Inner Ring Road (Figs. 1 and 2) and was once of more economic importance in the city. The Grosvenor Bridge long since diverted traffic from the Dee Bridge to which the main street of the area, Lower Bridge Street, leads. More recently, the busy junction of the Inner Ring Road at Pepper Street has also isolated the area somewhat. There are many good, large buildings of the eighteenth century and earlier which originally housed the wealthy as well as a number of later, more humble, terrace houses. Some houses were still used as homes in 1966 but many were empty, underused or doing duty as storage space. For example, there was an upholstery store in part of Gamul House and a tyre store in a large eighteenth century house, 25 Castle Street, while Shipgate House groaned under a weight of library books. Neglect over the years had taken its toll of many buildings and any incentive to repair was outweighed by uncertainty about the future and the threat of compulsory purchase under housing legislation or for an extension to County Hall. Complete redevelopment of two large sites in Lower Bridge Street was proposed and a new, vast and inelegant motor showroom already intruded on the historic scene as a portent of total change. It appeared that the blighting effects of neglect, uncertainty, disincentive to repair, and the lack of any reasonable economic use compounded the usual problems of buildings of unsuitable size for modern uses, lack of plumbing facilities, and the lack of rear access. Urgent attention was needed.

Encouraged by the Consultant, the Preservation Policy Group (which was anxious to see pilot action areas), and the Civic Trust, the City decided to treat the area as a pilot area for conservation action. This meant involving owners in several schemes at once. Hence a number of the rescue schemes already mentioned—Shipgate House, Tudor House and Gamul House—were taken up.

Much of the property in this area is more suited to residential use than anything else and the City is anxious to see it restored wherever possible. Housing is no longer a feature of the historic centre of Chester—indeed the 1966 studies showed a greater predominance of commercial uses in Chester than in other historic cities. Such residential use as there is, is largely confined to 'islands' near the Walls and in the Bridgegate Area.

In Bridgegate, however, some progress has been made but so far this has been principally in properties owned by the City. A nineteenth century courtyard and terrace of sixteen houses adjoining Gamul House are being rehabilitated. New housing is planned on the site of a relocated Salvation Army Citadel nearby and on the site of the former tyre store next to 25 Castle Street. These

0   150 FEET
0   50 METRES

1 GAMUL HOUSE
2 GAMUL PLACE
3 TUDOR HOUSE
4 25 CASTLE STREET
5 BRIDGE PLACE

REPAIR, USUALLY WITH CONVERSION OR IMPROVEMENT
BUILDINGS NOT INSPECTED OR FOUND SATISFACTORY
PRIVATE REDEVELOPMENT
LANDSCAPING PROPOSED

REDEVELOPMENT AFTER PURCHASE BY CITY COUNCIL
R RESIDENTIAL USE RECOMMENDED
O OFFICE USE RECOMMENDED

Fig. 2 Plan of the Bridgegate Action Area in Chester, showing the principal proposals for the area

sites are to be developed by Housing Associations. The County Council, in restoring Shipgate House, has converted the upper floor into flats; as already noted, Tudor House is a home. Unfortunately, it has not always been possible to restore the residential use and 25 Castle Street will very likely be used for offices, as are several other old houses.

Of the two new office developments proposed in Lower Bridge Street, that on the corner of Pepper Street is now building to approved designs; the other, after several years of negotiation, is still pending. It is hoped that a scheme will be worked out whereby the façade of the remaining buildings in Lower Bridge Street may be incorporated in the new building.

Environmental improvements by way of planting and resurfacing are proposed, but have not yet been made. One of the most obvious, and long talked of, is to prevent car parking in front of Bridge Place next to the Bridge Gate. This small space, with cobbles and row of trees, could set off the eighteenth century façade behind it to far greater advantage if it were refurbished. A very straightforward scheme to repair the surfaces and edges would serve.

As with the building restoration programme, progress in the Bridgegate Area is there to be seen, and as more schemes are completed the concentration of work, for example in the Gamul House, Place and Terrace schemes, will certainly heighten the impact and illustrate the benefits of a concerted attack on a variety of buildings with their restoration to different uses. The successes so far achieved, however, emphasize the magnitude of the task; the programme, though five years old, is yet in the early stages of implementation.

Sympathy between new development and its historic surrounding must be a major objective in any conservation area but it is notoriously difficult to define. Planners in Chester resisted the precise definition of the planning standards, elevational treatment, materials, etc. that they are looking for. Rather they have preferred to negotiate proposals for each site in the light of the unique problems it poses and the opportunities it offers. The wide variety of style and age in the existing buildings has given them good reason thus to keep options open and attempt, on the one hand, to explain the quality of development they hope will be attained and, on the other, to avoid a fight over the misapplication of their own standards.

Almost all the redevelopment which has taken place in the four principal shopping streets has been in Watergate Street where the gaps, so noticeable in 1966, have been filled. As with restoration, the fact that the new buildings do not jar, is in itself a measure of success, and, in fact, they do better than that, for they are elegant. That these developments have brought in new uses to help revive shopping in this street and have restored the continuity of the Rows are yet other measures of success. In other parts of the city centre, too, redevelopment during the past six or seven years of sites fronting to the main streets must be counted more sympathetic than some previous schemes. In several cases redevelopment has taken in a number of adjoining properties but the disasters of long horizontal lines along the new frontages, so obviously odd in a city of narrow fronted properties, have been avoided, most successfully perhaps in the C & A store in Foregate Street. Often redevelopment has included substantial building at the rear but this has been disguised by stepping back the roof line of the upper floors so that they are not seen from the main street. The general impression is of addition rather than outright change and the only strong criticism that this writer would make is of the area behind the Town Hall and to the north of Watergate Street which is entirely given over to modern buildings, mostly offices. Allowances have to be made, since one of these buildings is only recently completed and some old, rear properties are being demolished to make room for another, but it is difficult to see how the contrast between the human scale and interesting variety of the Rows and the bleak bulk of the new offices can ever strike as less than an environmental disaster in the setting of this historic city. Fortunately, the impact of the 'new' is lessened by the area being entirely cut off from the 'old' by the continuous frontages of the historic streets, penetrated only by footpaths.

The Conservation Area and Planning Policies

Conservation, however important, is but one aspect of planning policy. In this section, I shall first outline the major changes which have taken place in Chester since 1969.

The Conservation Area is largely given over to shopping and office uses. The shopping centre is very compact and occupies the four central streets at the heart of the walled city and the traditional market area in Foregate Street outside the East Gate. Private offices occupy many converted houses. The Town Hall in Northgate Street and the Castle and County Hall complex beside the River house some of the local authority and other government and administrative offices which are so important in Chester (Fig. 1).

Changes were taking place before the conservation programme began. The precinct form of shopping development fits particularly well with Chester's medieval streets, the Rows, where a second storey provides a safe, pedestrian, level of shops. Three were planned in the mid-1960s, and the first, the Grosvenor Laing precinct, so successfully fitted into the land behind the Rows of Eastgate and Bridge Street, was opened in 1965.[2] The Forum, which was part of a large office and shopping development beside the Town Hall, the new market Hall and Theatre, was building and a smaller precinct, Mercia Square, was planned. Three large office blocks had been built, one for the Police, opposite the Castle; the other two near the Town Hall were occupied by the County Council and a government department. (See Fig. 1 and Plate 6).

Chester is regarded as part of the North West Region of England; its regional position is, therefore, officially assessed in relation to Merseyside and Greater Manchester and the effects of change in the Welsh part of its hinterland are not considered. The latest essay in regional planning in the North West[3] shows that in the pursuit of rising personal standards people, especially those in middle and upper income groups, have moved to the southern margins of the conurbations. In the last few years the population of Wirral, the Cheshire villages, (and, incidentally, the Welsh shore of the Dee) has substantially increased. With sufficient land already allocated to residential use or carrying planning permission for housing in these areas to meet comfortably any predicted demand it seems likely that the population in the area from which Chester must draw its trade is likely to continue to grow and to include the more prosperous people of the Region.

The greater numbers of prosperous people living within easy reach of Chester must have been one factor in the growth of the shopping centre. Floor-space figures alone are, admittedly, an inadequate measure of growth but in the absence of the 1971 Census of Distribution may serve as an indication. In all some 410 000 sq. ft. (38 090 sq. m.) have been built since 1961 in the Conservation Area. Two types of development, which have taken place since 1966, account for rather more than 70 per cent of this. In the first place the three precincts provide 150 000 sq. ft. (13 935 sq. m.) all of which has been let, though not entirely without difficulty judging by circumstantial evidence such as the un-attractively blank windows of a large betting shop at the entrance to Mercia Square. In the second place, major national stores, among them C & A and Marks and Spencer, have built as much new space again in new stores or in extensions to existing stores in Foregate Street. Apart from these two develop-ments, there has been an increase in the number of small shops selling clothes, quality durable goods and antiques, the last probably a reflection of a growing tourist trade. These small shops have concentrated in the busier parts of the Rows which remain those in Eastgate Street and Bridge Street but they have also moved into Watergate Street and contributed to a welcome revival of trade there (Plate 2).

It is difficult to describe the recent changes in Chester's shopping centre more precisely than by saying that the evidence points to a rise in trade; that changes in the function of the shopping centre may be supposed since convenience goods have taken up only a small part of the new floor-space while there are more shops selling durable goods. In relation to conservation, the more important points are that, so far, the shopping centre remains firmly rooted in the historic core and that the continued prosperity of small shops seems to have contributed to the continued use of many old properties.

Offices have been built on an unprecedented scale in the past few years. More than 300 000 sq. ft. (27 870 sq. m.) were constructed in the city centre between 1961 and 1974 and, as in the case of new shops, the major part has been built since the middle of the 1960s. Employment in offices, the fastest growing sector of employment in the city, during this period increased by nearly 50 per cent. Much of the new space has been developed in speculative schemes, developers presumably influenced by the relatively prestigious location of a county town and the possibilities for good housing nearby. In the event, however, some two thirds has been occupied by government and local authority offices. Insurance, finance and banking are also represented. Considering the relatively small scale of the historic city centre so much development is of major importance and is by far the most noticeable change of recent years.

Rather more than one third of the new office space has been built over the shopping precincts, including one of the largest schemes, an extension to the Town Hall offices of 68 000 sq. ft. (6 317 sq. m.) over the Forum. One or two schemes, such as Refuge House in Watergate Street, combine the redevelopment of a small frontage with substantial development at the rear, but over half of the new office space is in new blocks located between Watergate Street, Northgate Street, Hunter Street and the Inner Ring Road. The effect has been to concentrate new development near the shopping centre and the bus station in Northgate Street, and where traffic can reach the new buildings directly from the Inner Ring Road or from Northgate Street.

Planning permission had been given for a further 246 000 sq. ft. (28 854 sq. m.) of offices and applications made for another 307 500 sq. ft. (28 567 sq. m.) when the Council decided, in 1974, to call a halt to further permission for two years so that they could assess the effect of such rapid expansion on the function and fabric of the city. The County Council is, of course, also involved in a question of such strategic importance. The most urgent consideration, inevitably, is that of traffic congestion.

In dealing with traffic congestion Chester has the advantage of an extremely compact business centre now encircled by an Inner Ring Road. This, completed in 1971, is not without its critics, for the western arm cuts through the walled city and isolates part of it. Moreover, the roundabouts in the northern section take up much land, yet need extra traffic controls at peak periods. Given current experience elsewhere, it must be a question whether the road would now find favour,[4] far less finance, but even those who begrudge space to the car must surely accept that the Inner Ring Road has brought very considerable benefits to the business centre. Apart from a reduction in the level of traffic throughout the central area, it has made it possible to restrict access to the four central streets to buses and essential traffic and only buses may traverse the Cross. A lot of space has been freed for pedestrians and this has brought a degree of relief from danger, noise and fumes which makes shopping in Chester a pleasant experience. This relief would equally benefit residents if, and when, it might be possible to convert the upper storeys of the old buildings to homes.

Many workers, as well as shoppers and visitors, travel in by car and a number of car parks have been built on the Inner Ring Road. There are some 7 500 parking spaces in the central area, two-thirds of them in public car parks. The City has recently become concerned at the number of commuters' cars taking up spaces and has altered the pricing system of two car parks distinctly in favour of short-stay visits. Public transport is part of the equation, of course, and questions about the rôle of the bus service and the routes buses should take through or round the central area are now the subject of public debate.

The Next Steps

As regards the historic centre, the questions which spring most readily to mind concern the location of further shopping and office developments, the management of the traffic they generate and their effect on the function of the city centre and consequently on the survival of the historic buildings and environment.

Opportunities for complete redevelopment present themselves most clearly in the north east between the Inner Ring Road and the Walls. Here, the new road cuts across the 'grain' of former streets and a good deal of land has been cleared. There is a minimum of historic buildings to cater for and the adjoining section of the Inner Ring Road, not yet carrying its 'practical' capacity at peak periods, would cater for traffic generated by new development. Several proposals are under discussion. Planning permission has been granted for office development of 73 000 sq. ft. (6 781 sq. m.) on the island site at the eastern extremity of the Inner Ring Road. A comprehensive scheme is under discussion which includes a new shopping precinct twice the size of the Grosvenor Laing precinct, a hotel and conference centre between the Canal and the Inner Ring Road and some housing on a third site. All these developments would link into the existing pattern of footpaths and vehicular circulation, but it must be a question whether such large scale development in this part of the town would pull the business centre, particularly the shopping centre, well to the east and endanger the survival of the shops which use the Rows, and whether it would absorb so much investment and effort as to discourage investment in the historic city.

A more attractive site to the conservationist for the next development might be the back land to the west of Bridge Street and the south of Watergate Street where there is the alluring prospect that a shopping precinct would encourage trade in the adjoining Rows as successfully as the Grosvenor Laing precinct did in those opposite. Site difficulties would be greater here, inevitably, as the new buildings would have to knit into the historic frontage and other existing property. Under current proposals for the site the total shopping and office space would be considerably smaller. However, the offices as well as shops, would enjoy proximity to others and would be well served by buses, though traffic generated would be likely to use the busiest, southern section of the Inner Ring Road.

Whether or not investment in housing in the Conservation Area will materialize must remain a matter of conjecture. There are the hopeful signs in Bridgegate and in a trickle of planning applications, notably one for seventy-two flats near the western Wall. The City now encourages developers to include housing in package schemes for commercial development and, again, there is hope of future success.

The next developments in traffic management in the central area are another matter for debate. Many properties in the four main shopping streets lack rear access so that deliveries must be catered for at some period during the day. The next question is to decide the balance of advantages between bringing people right into the centre by bus and allowing for all routes to converge in Northgate Street and, on the other hand, running buses through streets otherwise given over to pedestrians. This is not simply a question of accessibility and the quality of public transport against the possible danger of accidents but also a question of environment. Bustle and activity are part of the shopping scene; people alone may not provide quite enough so that in some settings other activities are needed or the space must be confined. In Chester there is already a pedestrian level of shopping above the street and part of the attraction of the Rows lies in the contrast they afford with the busy street below. There may well be advantages in retaining some vehicles to point the contrast. Restrictions to cars have not been long in force and the City's policy is to proceed step by step and consider the results of each experiment.

Whether it is decided to route buses through or round the shopping centre, street paving will need to be redesigned to make the most of the improvements in reduced levels of traffic. This poses the usual problems of the sensitive design of the signals of restraint. Will Chester, for example, be able to solve the problem of restraining traffic without the lavish use of yellow paint?

Conclusions

What conclusions are to be drawn from this review of the first years of Chester's conservation programme? The record shows that something like ten times as much public money is being spent this year than in the first year of the programme. The restored buildings are there to see, in use or shortly to be opened. The city has seen a period of prosperity perhaps greater than might have been expected in the late 1960s, but the development that prosperity has brought has, so far, been absorbed. The general historic setting remains domestic, vernacular, and intimate in scale yet thoroughly appropriate to the last quarter of the twentieth century in a town of this size and function. There is nothing of the museum piece about the historic city. So far, the first stages of the conservation programme must be counted an undoubted success. Yet the problems which seem most in need of attention in the next stages of the programme have a familiar ring, concerned as they still must be with the problems of providing incentives to private owners to invest in old buildings, of finding economic uses for the whole of the old buildings, of maintaining their fabric and their setting in an uncertain economic climate and of ensuring the future economic prosperity of the historic parts of the city while redeveloping adjacent areas which are cleared or underused.

NOTES AND REFERENCES

1 Insall, Donald and Associates, *Chester: A Study in Conservation*, London, HMSO, 1968.

2 Tasker, Sidney H., 'Chester: The Challenge of Change', *Town Planning Review*, Vol. 37, No. 3, (October 1966), pp. 189–206.

3 North West Joint Planning Team, *The Strategic Plan for the North West*, London, HMSO, 1974.

4 Worskett, Roy, 'Great Britain: Progress in Conservation', *Architectural Review*, No. 935, (January 1975), p. 14.

ADDITIONAL REFERENCES

Tilley, Roger, 'Conservation in Action in Chester', *Built Environment*, (May 1973), pp. 287–289.

Insall, Donald, 'Action for Conservation: Chester', *Journal of the Royal Town Planning Institute*, Vol. 56, No. 7, (July/August 1970).

Green, A., *Conservation—More than Preservation*, unpublished MCD paper, University of Liverpool, 1974.

Pamphlets issued by Chester City Council at various dates.

Edinburgh

An experiment in positive conservation

ANN MacEWEN

Nowhere else in the world is there a complete classical city like the New Town of Edinburgh. In its extent and completeness it has no rival. It is an expression of the Enlightenment—one of the great eras of civilization in which there was confidence in human progress and in the power of reason, and to which Scotsmen such as David Hume, Adam Smith and James Watt can boast a major contribution. In describing the early nineteenth century extension to the New Town which had begun in the 1760s, Henry Russell Hitchcock says:

'The result rivals Petersburg (i.e. Leningrad) as well as Copenhagen, Berlin and Munich. Indeed, in Edinburgh, what was built between 1760 and 1860 provides the most extensive example of romantic classical architecture in the world.'[1]

What is more, with about three quarters of its 11 750 properties in residential use, the New Town is still largely used as it was designed to be used some 150 to 200 years ago—for living in. For these, and for other reasons I shall touch on, the New Town places Edinburgh in a class by itself—nationally and internationally —as a historic city. It is also in a class of its own in the United Kingdom in terms of the sheer size of the conservation problem it presents. But time, the elements and inadequate maintenance have taken their toll in all historic places, and in Edinburgh's New Town the investment needed for a renewed life of, say, another 100 years not only far exceeds the pockets of many owners, but inhibits local authority action also.

Even though it is unique as built and living history, not everyone likes Edinburgh's New Town. When walking round it with colleagues some years ago, I remember my surprise at discovering that, while they supported the case for preserving it, not all of them really thought it was a very attractive place. They found its formal layout, wide streets and classical buildings forbidding, grey and monotonous. They would not have wished to live in the New Town. Although I took a different view, and know many people who not only live in the New Town but love it, I had to admit that there were Edinburgh people who shared their feelings. Furthermore, for some the New Town symbolizes privilege— and the efforts of a dedicated minority to secure its repair and conservation are seen simply as the well-to-do pulling strings to get improvements to their own already well-endowed territory at public expense, while underprivileged areas in Edinburgh deteriorate still further.

Whatever one may think of these views, there appears to be no doubt that, without the considerable voluntary effort of a relatively few concerned people,

D

the central and local government funds now available (for a limited period) for restoration in the New Town would not have been forthcoming. As it is, the active conservation of the New Town is just getting off to a very good start and is the focus of Heritage Year attention. But it is only the start of a twenty-year programme. Whether the effort can be sustained and extended to the conservation of the whole of the New Town and to other parts of the city will depend, in an era of restriction on public spending, on the extent of local support for conservation. The broader based this is, the greater are the chances that the central and local government funds essential to the implementation of the programme will be forthcoming.

Description

The New Town was built in stages, starting in 1767 as an extension to the Old Town, essentially for the new bourgeoisie. The Old Town had become desperately overcrowded, but peripheral expansion was impossible because medieval Edinburgh was built on a sloping ridge with steep sides, having the castle on its rock at its west end and Holyrood Palace at its east. The bold step taken in the second half of the eighteenth century was to drain the Nor' Loch on the north side of the Old Town ridge, to throw the North bridge across the valley, and to start building a residential suburb in the classical style on the lower, more gently sloping ridge on the other side (Plate 8).

The New Town took 80 years or so to build, and the saga of this great enterprise has been marvellously told by Professor A. J. Youngson.[2] He observes that it was the interests and ambitions of the merchant and professional middle class of Edinburgh that drove forward the city's extraordinary advance from the middle of the eighteenth century. At this time there was a need to stem the drift of the wealthy to London by a programme of planned expansion, which would both make Edinburgh a more attractive place in which to live and encourage commercial growth.

The idea of a New Town was first publicly promoted in 1752 by the city fathers of the day and its development took place in three main phases (Fig. 1). In 1766 a competition for the layout plan was won by the young architect, James Craig. The first phase of development—sometimes called Craig's New Town and sometimes called the first New Town—was based on Craig's plan and consists in essence of three great parallel axes, Princes, George and Queen Streets, and two squares—Charlotte (designed by Robert Adam) and St. Andrews. Towards the end of the eighteenth century St. James Square was designed by James Craig as an eastward extension of the first New Town. It was demolished in 1966 to make way for large-scale office development which both in scale and detail is a disastrous intrusion into classical Edinburgh. The commercial pressures of the late nineteenth and twentieth centuries have caused the almost complete replacement of the original buildings in Princes Street, and of many in George Street. As a result Craig's New Town and the St. James Square area are now the commercial, financial and professional hub of the city, and indeed of Scotland. Unhappily the imagination and enterprise that in the eighteenth century both

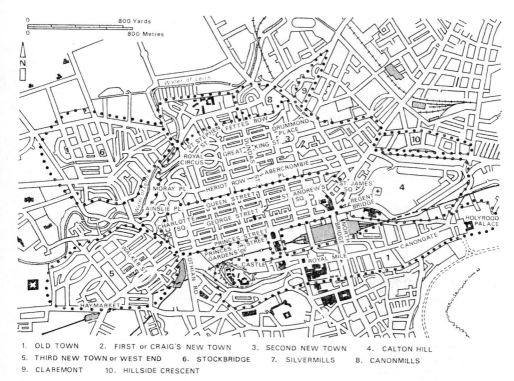

1. OLD TOWN   2. FIRST or CRAIG'S NEW TOWN   3. SECOND NEW TOWN   4. CALTON HILL
5. THIRD NEW TOWN or WEST END   6. STOCKBRIDGE   7. SILVERMILLS   8. CANONMILLS
9. CLAREMONT   10. HILLSIDE CRESCENT

Fig. 1. Plan, showing the development of the New Town of Edinburgh in three main stages together with later extensions

stimulated the economic growth of Edinburgh and directed development to new locations, have been missing from the control of similar pressures in the second half of the twentieth century and Craig's New Town has suffered (Plates 8-11).

In the early nineteenth century a second 'New Town' got under way, separated from the first by the beautiful slopes of Queen Street gardens. The area was designed by Reid and Sibbald on the northward slope of the New Town ridge. With Great King Street linking Royal Circus to Drummond Place, the layout echoes the east-west axial treatment of Craig's New Town, but is less formal in character, and contains some of the finest domestic architecture of the New Town.

To the east of the second New Town proper is Calton Hill and the development of this area, incorporating the Regent Bridge which links the east end of Princes Street to Calton Hill, was started after 1812. Great terraces and gardens skirt the lower eastern slopes of Calton Hill, and monuments crown the Hill itself forming a dramatic group as seen from Princes Street. But the more ambitious plans to extend the Calton Hill scheme to Leith were never realized.

In the 1820s the relatively small and steeply sloping area to the north-west of the first New Town was developed. Owned by the Earl of Moray and known as the Moray Estate, a scheme for interlinked crescents, terraces and a circus was designed by Gillespie Graham in the grand classical manner. The Moray Estate and Calton Hill areas are commonly thought of together with Reid and Sibbald's extension as the second New Town.

The last great achievement known as the third New Town, or the West End, lies to the west of Charlotte Square. It was started in the 1820s, but building continued broadly on classical lines well into the Victorian era. Finally, there are the fringe developments of the New Town. Across the Water of Leith, Edinburgh's secret and neglected river, lie streets of smaller scale houses at Stockbridge. And to the north and east of the second New Town are isolated extensions at Silvermills, Canonmills, Claremont and Hillside Crescent.

All this covers some 700 acres and today some 24 300 people live in the New Town out of a total Edinburgh population of about 462 000. To the south of the Old and New Towns lie Tollcross and Southside, important districts whose renewal policies are under review (Fig. 2).

How could anyone find the New Town dull? The superimposition of formal streets and squares, crescents and circuses on the hilly terrain in itself produces interest and diversity. To this is added the contrast between the grass and trees of the formal gardens and the stone of the surrounding buildings; the surprise interruptions of the gridiron layout caused by estate boundaries and old routes; the rich variety of architectural detail and ironwork (Plate 10); the exploitation of basements with their wide and sometimes very deep areas and flights of steps soaring over to link pavement to front door; the range of house types—from aristocrat to artisan—reflecting the hierarchical nature of the society of the day; the drama of the Water of Leith which runs in a wooded ravine along the northern edge of the second New Town, and of Telford's bridge over it; and the breathtaking view from the ridge of the first New Town in George Street northwards across the Firth of Forth to the hills of Fife beyond, and southwards to the crenallated skyline of the castle and the Old Town. To cap it all there is Princes Street, which despite its international fame is now mediocre architecturally and popular rather than exclusive as a shopping street. But where else is there anything in the world to compare to the views from Princes Street of the neo-Acropolis on Calton Hill, and the North Bridge spanning the valley; of Princes Street Gardens with their exuberant Scott Monument in the gothic style, their statues and their concealed railway where the Nor' Loch used to be; of Playfair's classical buildings on the Mound, and above of the grim and romantic castle on its rock and the profile of the Old Town buildings seemingly piled one on top of the other up to the ridge. From Princes Street, the coexistence of the new classical town alongside the old mediaeval one is there for all to see, a relationship that supports Edinburgh's claim to be unique amongst cities. Edinburgh's history can be read almost like an open book (Plate 13).

Inside the buildings of the New Town there is yet more interest to be found. Although the terraces appear to consist of individual dwellings, many of them are in fact made up of flats. The tenement of several storeys was a characteristic of the cramped living conditions of the Old Town. Inside these tall buildings it was the privileged who lived in the flats on the middle floors, and humbler families who lived above and below. This traditional demand for flats was an important influence in the design of terraces in the New Town. Although the

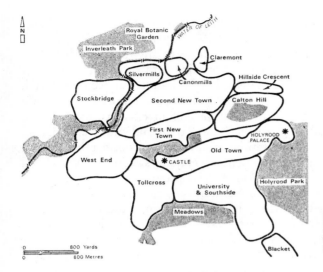

Fig. 2 Diagrammatic plan of central Edinburgh. Showing the main areas of that part of the city and, shaded, areas of open space

second half of the eighteenth century was a time of economic expansion, there was a disparity between the scale of the grander classical terraces that were to rival London, and the ability of the Scottish bourgeoisie and noblemen, for whom the New Town accommodation was intended, to pay for and run a complete house from basement to attic. Scottish ingenuity triumphed, and many of the terraces that look as though they were made up of individual houses in fact incorporate flats in the centre of the terrace and at the ends (with vertical class segregation as in the Old Town tenements), and separate houses in between. These original sub-divisions have presumably facilitated the retention of New Town buildings in residential use, but as over 70 per cent of the dwellings are owner-occupied, the arrangement does complicate the business of repairs and maintenance.

Conservation

Preservation of buildings and conservation are well-established principles in Edinburgh, and a number of factors have acted together to give the New Town both its integrated form and buildings that last. From the start terraces were built by individual developers, but in conformity with design and other require-ments laid down by the feudal superior, and this practice was enforced throughout the construction of the whole New Town. To this can be added, the strict code of building regulations enforced by the Dean of Guild, the essential durability of the local stone from the Craigleith quarries, and the structural stability of the buildings themselves. Unfortunately not all the buildings in the New Town are built in enduring Craigleith stone, and there is much deterioration of wall and decorative features. But the New Town, unlike Nash's jerry-building in London, was built to last. Perhaps the Scots had a shrewder eye for a long-term investment.

Edinburgh's first scheme of area conservation (as opposed to restoration of individual buildings) was for Canongate, in the eastern part of the Royal Mile in the Old Town. Starting in the 1950s old buildings were rehabilitated and new ones built in character to give a new lease of life to an historic street. With the 1960s came pressure for commercial and other development in many parts of Edinburgh and with it the tall building as the easy answer to problems of plot ratio and daylighting, not to mention prestige and advertisement. Not before some schemes which now spoil the Edinburgh skyline had been approved, the City Corporation commissioned from Lord Holford a report on the siting of high buildings which was published in 1968. This in effect ruled out high buildings in or immediately adjacent to the New Town and must have played a part in persuading the City Corporation to reverse (at considerable cost) a previous decision to approve a development at Haymarket in the West End that would have dominated this area. Commercial pressures to redevelop sites in Craig's New Town caused much concern and in 1967 the Princes Street Panel, a professional panel appointed by the City Corporation, produced a policy report for the whole first New Town area. New development is accordingly subject to limitations of height, plot ratio and materials. However, the somewhat high plot ratio of 3½:1 combined with the Panel's provisions for an elevated walkway in Princes Street and its apparent disregard for the quality of George Street have resulted in some new buildings that disfigure the New Town.

After the Civic Amenities Act 1967, a number of studies of possible conservation areas were undertaken by the City Planning Department. Of these, eight are in the New Town but only two—St. Andrews (consisting of the first New Town apart from Princes Street, the second New Town, the Moray Estate), and Calton Hill—have been designated. The aim is to designate the remainder during Heritage Year. Outside the New Town, Blacket (the Georgian suburb to the south of the Old Town), has been designated and the villages of Swanston and Duddingston have been studied. The most serious omission, of course, is the medieval Old Town.

The tide of the New Town's fortunes turned in 1970. A conference on the New Town inspired by Sir Robert Matthew and organized by the Civic Trust and the Edinburgh Architectural Association was held. The critical feature of the conference was the presentation of a voluntary study carried out by members of the Edinburgh Architectural Association of the fabric of the New Town. This had taken a year of spare-time work and put the cost over 20 years of restoring stonework, roofs, chimneys, doors, windows, below-ground areas and railings at £15 million (at 1970 prices). The study did not cover the interiors of buildings. The conference, which was fully reported,[3] achieved its object in extracting from the Secretary of State for Scotland the necessary promise of financial help. A special New Town Conservation Committee was set up in 1971 and a full-time director, Desmond Hodges, was appointed in 1972.

Edinburgh City Corporation has been reluctant to designate conservation areas, to give grants towards the maintenance of listed buildings, or to spend money in any way, because it feared that with so much to preserve, conservation would be a vast drain on the City's resources. It was only when, as the result of public pressure, the government made a special three-year contribution towards the care of the New Town that the City developed a more positive approach.

With the publication in 1972 of the final report of the Planning and Transport

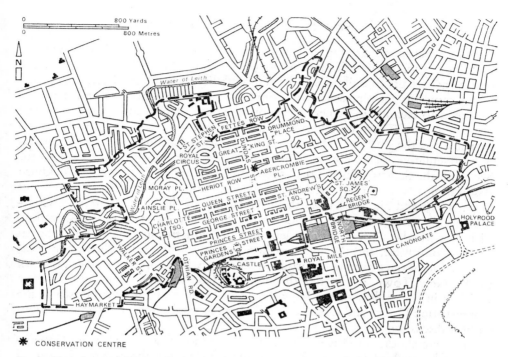

Fig. 3 Plan of central Edinburgh, showing the boundary of the conservation area (broken line) and the location of the conservation centre

Study,[4] the northern part of the New Town, and other areas around the centre including the Meadows, were reprieved from the threat of a possible Inner Ring Road. However, some of the main recommendations of the 1972 report have themselves proved contentious, in particular new road links further out than the Inner Ring Road, intended to deflect non centre-bound traffic away from the New and Old Towns and the University district to the south; and a road tunnel under Charlotte Square linking the west end of Queen Street to Lothian Road, which would relieve the Square and Princes Street, but increase traffic in Queen Street.

The public transport proposals of the report for a much-improved bus system have been subjected to a further study by new consultants in which yet more investigation of light rail as the answer is recommended.[5] But other recommendations of the 1972 study for management schemes to keep extraneous traffic out of the New Town, and to close Princes Street—or part of it—to all vehicles except buses and service vans, are being considered for implementation. Parking regulations that favour residents have been introduced in certain parts of the New Town, but after seven years of combined study and deliberation there is still no integrated planning and transport policy for Edinburgh; and no comprehensive proposals for access and environment in the New Town covering traffic control, car storage, pedestrian movement and parking, in the context of which conservation policies—for new buildings, rehabilitation, gardens, back areas and so on—can be developed.

The New Town Conservation Committee

Planning, transport, housing and conservation policies for the New Town rest with the City Corporation (since May 1975 a District Council). The programme of external repairs to buildings is the responsibility of the New Town Conservation Committee, a representative Committee with an independent Chairman. Its aim is to encourage owners to restore the entire fabric and original external features of New Town buildings over the next twenty years, and to make grants available for the purpose. The Committee is not a Corporation one. It consists of representatives of Edinburgh Corporation, the Historic Buildings Council for Scotland, the Scottish Civic Trust, the Scottish Georgian Society, the Cockburn Association, New Town Residents' Associations, the Scottish Development Department and Sir Robert Matthew, Chairman of the 1970 Conference Committee and, until last year, adviser to the Secretary of State on conservation. Liaison with the Corporation is achieved through the six councillors who sit on the Committee, and through collaboration at officer level with the conservation section of the planning department. Contact with people who live and work in the New Town is fostered through the Conservation Committee's office which is in the middle of the New Town in Dundas Street. It is known as the Conservation Centre and is used regularly for meetings of owners, for exhibitions and for discussions (Fig. 3).

Funds are allocated to the Committee in the ratio of two-thirds from Government and one-third from the Local Authority. For the three-year trial period 1972–1975 this has amounted to £75 000 for the first year (£50 000 Government and £25 000 Edinburgh Corporation), and £150 000 a year for the second and third years (£100 000 Government, £50 000 Edinburgh Corporation). The grants in general are in inverse ratio to the average net annual valuation of the block under repair, with an additional percentage payable if the conservation work is carried out through a Street Association or similar co-operative body. By paying higher rates of grant for the lower rated property the Committee is aiming to give more help to the poorer homes without the need for an invidious means test. Anything from new door furniture to the refacing of an entire elevation is encouraged; but always with the object of making a lasting improvement to the building which will encourage others to do likewise.

The New Town has been selected as one of the four UK 'Pilot Projects' for European Architectural Heritage Year 1975, and the aim is to complete a number of significant schemes by then. In its first two years of active life—mid-1972–1974 —the New Town Committee has concentrated on securing the edges of the New Town, where the deterioration of the fabric is most marked, against creeping decay and demolition. This was the policy suggested by the 1970 Conference, and most of the major schemes due for completion in 1975 are along the northern boundary of the second New Town (Plate 12). In the Committee's area between 30 and 40 street associations have been set up, and by the middle of 1975 it is expected that grants of over £300 000 will be firmly committed representing all of the public funds available to the Committee up to this date. It certainly looks, therefore, as though the Committee has achieved its first objective of setting up a programme of voluntary conservation by owners assisted by grants from public funds. Indeed grants already proposed in principle indicate that the annual public fund of £150 000 will have to be at least trebled to £450 000 if the programme is to be kept going.

There are problems, of course. The Master of Works (the City Surveyor) has an independent duty to demolish buildings or features which he considers dangerous, whether they are listed or not and without reference to other authorities. The City Council has been reluctant so far to acquire properties in the interests of conservation, although powers have existed for some time and new ones, under the Town and Country Amenities Act 1974, are now available to enable the local authority to do this. About 600 dwellings out of a total of 8 000 in the New Town area are empty. They fall into three categories— properties for sale, properties acquired by Edinburgh Corporation that will be renovated and added to the housing stock, and dwellings that have been closed because they are insanitary and cannot be re-opened until the owners have been persuaded to bring them up to standard or the new District Council take them over. Some poor owners in substandard properties are unable to pay their share of a comprehensive scheme of conservation. To overcome this difficulty the New Town Conservation Committee could perhaps use funds on a revolving basis to acquire properties in need of restoration whose owners cannot, or will not, take part in a conservation scheme, as has been successfully practised by the National Trust in Fife. Finally, there is the problem that some owners (mainly of commercial property) do not show interest in the conservation programme although they could well afford to co-operate. The support of owners is essential to the success of the conservation experiment in the New Town, and this attitude has prejudiced some joint schemes involving commercial and residential owners and thwarted others. Means will have to be found to bring these recalcitrant owners into line if the New Town is to be protected from their selfishness or indifference.

Perhaps the most intractable problem is in places where buildings have architectural value, but the structural condition of some is considered dangerous and the internal arrangements of others are below standards specified under the Housing Acts. Under normal procedures owners must repair the structure, demolish, or upgrade the accommodation as the case may be. Failure to comply brings the threat of immediate evacuation and demolition in the case of the dangerous structure, and compulsory acquisition by the local authority in order to renovate or demolish in the case of substandard accommodation. But compulsory acquisition, even for renovation, usually means that the families are re-housed elsewhere, with the result that the community is broken up and the incentive to renovate is weakened. St. Stephen Street to the north-west of the second New Town is just such a place. But, as Desmond Hodges explained to the local amenity society earlier this year, there are strong social, architectural and economic reasons why the normal course of events should be resisted in this area. His argument, based on the findings of a report specially commissioned by the Conservation Committee, was that community ties are long-established in the St. Stephen Street area; that the streets in question form an architectural link within the second New Town as a whole; and that the buildings themselves constitute valuable housing stock. Their restoration (though costly) would be cheaper than demolition and re-housing.

At the time of writing this chapter (March 1975) the future of St. Stephen Street hangs in the balance. Desmond Hodges sees the answer in the formation of a co-operative Housing Association which under recent legislation could acquire and renovate dwellings and re-let them to their former owners. But, as he told the amenity society, the essential prerequisite is that the St. Stephen Street residents should form themselves into a strong representative body which, together with representatives of the new Edinburgh District Council, the Conservation Committee and the Scottish Development Department, would form a Development Committee for the area. The main job for the Development Committee would be to agree a long-term plan covering the immediate repair and restoration of valuable buildings, proposals for suitable new buildings where necessary, and recommendations—after discussions with owners, developers, housing associations and the district council—on how the plan is to be financed and carried out. I hope this gets off the ground.

In the case of St. Stephen Street, the Conservation Committee and its director are taking a broad view of conservation and are playing the key role in an attempt to bend the bureaucratic processes of local government and to secure the integration of housing, dangerous structure and conservation policies for the area. If the residents and the Committee succeed, local people who want to go on living in the St. Stephen Street area will have better homes and a valuable corner of the New Town will have been restored.

The new housing legislation throws up another possibility for the poorer parts of the New Town like St. Stephen Street. They can be designated as Housing Action Areas which attract generous grants of 75 per cent-90 per cent to bring dwellings up to standard. If these funds were made available for external renovation as well as for interior improvement, it would greatly ease the pressure on the Conservation Committee's slender resources.

Popular Support for Conservation

At the beginning of this chapter I touched on the issue of popular support for conservation and the need to stimulate it. This is what European Architectural Heritage Year is all about, and Edinburgh's New Town is an interesting case study around which to discuss the question: who benefits from all the expenditure of public money on the conservation of the New Town? It can be argued that apart from Princes Street and George Street, the New Town is neither a great centre of activity for Edinburgh people as a whole, nor a great tourist attraction either. The beneficiaries are mainly the present residents and users and—perhaps more important—posterity. People need to understand that those who are alive today are custodians of the New Town for a short time only. They have a responsibility to pass it on in good shape so that future generations can learn from it and delight in it just as past generations have done. To allow piecemeal disintegration and redevelopment in the New Town simply because much of it is not of mass interest in Edinburgh would be equivalent to allowing the national archives or the paintings in the National Gallery to rot on the grounds that they appeal only to a small section of the British public. But the New Town is not a museum kept up entirely by the state or the municipality. It is a masterpiece of lived-in architecture that will survive only if looked after by its occupiers with the help of public money.

Needless to say, a wider interest in the New Town and other historic parts of Edinburgh would be very desirable. Clearly, the more the interest the more the support for conservation and the more likely it is that owners will cherish their property and that public funds will be forthcoming. But at a more fundamental level, people could themselves gain so much from a better understanding of the past through the monuments, streets and buildings of earlier times in which Edinburgh is so rich. These artefacts can bring to life events, people and ideas of past eras and thereby enrich understanding of the present; and there is also so much to be learnt from them about the art of creating civilized surroundings in which to live.

This suggests that historic and beautiful places need to be explained and interpreted to people and to play a bigger part in their lives. The National Trust is furnishing and decorating No. 7 Charlotte Square as it was originally and is opening it to the public as a contribution to European Architectural Heritage Year and this will certainly demonstrate to a wider group of people the quality of New Town houses. But is there not scope for something more ambitious by way of an interpretation centre-cum-museum for the New Town? The Conservation Committee's headquarters in Dundas Street fulfils this function to some degree and is a hive of activity at the moment, but perhaps a special centre is justified to which students, school children, adult groups, and tourist visitors could come to learn about the New Town before exploring it on the ground, perhaps by means of planned town trails. Talks and conducted tours are organized now by Edinburgh societies such as the Cockburn Association, and maybe these activities should be left in the hands of volunteers. Even so, a centre that would tell the story of the New Town, and provide a base from which to operate and campaign could help the cause of conservation.

It can also be argued that if citizens as a whole were able to get more out of the New Town, they might give more active support to the expenditure of public funds on its conservation. The possibility of allowing public access to the formal gardens (which are accessible at the moment only to fee-paying householders) has long been in my mind, ever since, in fact, the days of the Planning and Transport Study with which I was involved five years ago. In the course of the work a number of new road and underground car parking proposals were being canvassed that threatened the continuing existence of certain New Town squares and gardens as we know them. I remember feeling how much stronger the case for their preservation would have been had it been possible to say that they were widely used and enjoyed by the public. It is very frustrating to walk along Heriot Row or Queen Street and to be excluded from gardens whose empty joys can only be guessed at by peering through the railings. The counter-argument is, of course, that opening the gardens to the public would reduce the quality and the upkeep, and that maintenance costs are already a burden on the separate voluntary committees whose responsibility upkeep is. Certainly, public use would suggest a contribution from the local authority and a long-term management plan for the New Town gardens.

Conservation might also get more popular support, and be considered less of an elitist activity, if people with the professional know-how to put pressure on officialdom took an interest in the underprivileged parts of towns, as well as in the areas of special architectural and historic quality. In addition to helping the people in deprived areas to gain much needed attention and funds, might not such involvement create an opportunity to spread concern for the heritage and secure a wider base for cherishing it? At City Council level the commitment of funds to conservation is to an extent being balanced by the recent setting up of an Urban Deprivation Unit with limited funds to do something for the people in three problem areas. I feel very strongly that policies and programmes for conserving what is physically good and improving what is socially bad in urban conditions must go forward together. To concentrate on one to the exclusion of the other would heighten conflict and inhibit action on both fronts.

So, when it comes to assessing the actual achievements of the New Town experiment in conservation, I would suggest that the amount spent in grants, the number of buildings repaired, street associations set up and joint schemes developed are not the only criteria of success. To these must be added others concerned with community and social objectives, and with the spread of popular support for conserving the New Town. Without something to show in these directions (and it looks as though there may be) the great impetus given to conservation by the setting up of the Conservation Committee and by Heritage Year may not be sustainable. However, the biggest danger of all is that the Conservation Committee may stimulate the demand for conservation grants to new levels, just at the very moment when government and the local authorities are bent on curbing expenditure. This would turn European Architectural Heritage Year into a cruel farce. The whole idea of the pilot projects—of which Edinburgh New Town is one—is that, if successful, the project itself can continue and develop, and the experience gained can be applied elsewhere. For Edinburgh, Heritage Year will have failed unless its pilot project paves the way for the positive conservation not only of the whole of the New Town, but of the Old Town and Southside and the remainder of the city's architectural heritage.

NOTES AND REFERENCES

1 Hitchcock, Henry Russell, *Architecture: Nineteenth and Twentieth Centuries*, Harmondsworth, Middlesex, Penguin History of Art, 1958.

2 Youngson, A. J., *The Making of Classical Edinburgh*, Edinburgh, Edinburgh University Press, 1966.

3 *The Conservation of Georgian Edinburgh*, Edinburgh, Edinburgh University Press, 1972.

4 *Planning and Transport Study, Final Report 1972*, London, Colin Buchanan and Partners/ Freeman Fox and Associates.

5 *A Review of the Public Transport Elements of the Recommended Plan, Final Report 1975*, Edinburgh, De Leuw Chadwick and O. hEocha.

Historic gardens and landscapes

The conservation of a national asset

LAURENCE J. FRICKER

Our desire to conserve the physical residues of the past is, I suggest, partially motivated by a wish to appreciate as much of the context of other people's lives as we possibly can. Architecture is a large part of that context and in that some aspects of our landscape are included during a year in which we are invited to acknowledge our European architectural heritage it is clear that in some way they are part of architecture's context. In 1964 the International Council of Monuments and Sites (ICOMOS) issued from Venice a declaration of its contexual scope. The concept of an historic monument embraces not only the single architectural work but also the urban or rural setting in which is found the evidence of a particular civilization, a significant development or an historic event. This applies not only to great works of art but also to more modest works of the past which have acquired cultural significance with the passing of time. This declaration is by no means a definition, for there are certainly difficulties in defining a landscape, a garden, a landscape garden, and what special reasons constitute their being historic. Almost any landscape or tract of country offers evidence, in some form or other, of the uses to which it has been put by man which is why historical geographers quite properly refer to the landscape as a palimpsest.[1]

These problems of definition were highlighted during 1974 when the Garden History Society, which figures largely in this article, was urgently active in its attempt to establish a national policy in Britain for the protection of historic gardens and landscapes. Discussion with the Institute of Landscape Architects resulted in a suggestion from Bodfan Gruffydd that an Historic Landscapes Council should be set up to protect and maintain historic landscapes of national importance, following the model of the Historic Buildings Council. There were practical parliamentary reasons why this was not pursued, but one might assume that attempts to find a precise definition which describes the Cerne Abbas Giant in Dorset as accurately as Gertrude Jekyll's own garden[2] proved more difficult than defining architecture. Because of these difficulties of definition and the need to narrow the scope of this chapter, I shall restrict myself to those parts of the British landscape which we call gardens. Gardens, referring to historic gardens, are discussed in relation to the aims of conservation, the establishment of a Garden History Society and the development of legislation within the planning sphere to preserve the gardens for posterity. Finally, this chapter makes a plea for the better management of historic gardens and concludes by suggesting that since gardens have a dynamic content, it is the style of gardening that should be protected as well as the gardens themselves.

THE AIMS OF CONSERVATION IN RELATION TO HISTORIC GARDENS

In 1967 the International Federation of Landscape Architects (IFLA) set up an historical section, the aims of which were as follows:

1. The establishment of a list of gardens of historical interest throughout the world;
2. The making of an attempt to find the necessary means for protecting, conserving and restoring those recognized as worthy of attention, and arranging for their upkeep;
3. The examination and recording in writing of the rules to be observed by those in charge of these gardens, with regard both to architectural design and to the plants to be grown and their settings and immediate surroundings;
4. The adoption of energetic measures to prevent the destruction of gardens thus qualifying for protection.

These aims were seen to be so similar to those of ICOMOS that the two organizations decided to hold an international symposium—the first of its kind—on the conservation and restoration of gardens of historic interest. Speakers were invited to address the symposium on the particular way in which the topic was understood in the country which they were invited to represent. The symposium was held at Fontainebleau in September, 1971 and was attended by delegates from Italy, France, Czechoslovakia, United Kingdom, West Germany, Belgium, USSR Hungary, Spain, Sweden and Japan.

The Belgian landscape architect and chairman of the Historical Section of IFLA was René Pérchère. He had first suggested the symposium and was its chief rapporteur and organizer. In his opening address at Fontainebleau he adopted the familiar defensive attitude of the professional. For example; 'while a garden is unquestionably the joint work of a designer and a gardener'; and 'each country, it is true, has its traditions. However, each age has its basic rules and a given style to which all must conform'; and, of significant interest—'my own personal "garden bible" is in three volumes namely Vaux-le-Vicomte, Granada, and the Villa Lante.'[3] This last statement is significant because for Pérchère, the future of the landscape profession would be greatly threatened if the future of those three famous gardens were not guaranteed. He argued that while the present task of landscape architects is to take more responsibility for environmental welfare and design than is contained even by the boundaries of Versailles, the professional and public, on whose behalf he works, share, or should do so, a common cultural heritage. In short, designers must be better trained and the public better educated.

The difference may be between the professional and amateur, the educated and uneducated. And although we are not overdisposed to acknowledge the cultural contribution of the latter, I would suggest that in discussing British gardens it is as significant as the former's. The fact that Pérchère does not acknowledge these differences is partly explained by the fact that he is a professional landscape architect and also that his traditional inheritance (note well, his reference to Vaux-le-Vicomte, Granada, Villa Lante) lead him to define the garden differently from the way we do in Britain. What is a garden? Is it made by nature? 'I personally', says Pérchère, 'have always answered that Nature, in fact, does not make gardens. The British will tell you: "A garden, for us, is where man seeks to find his place in Nature". And to this I always reply· "For me, a garden is where man marks out his place in nature."' Pérchère would generously have us all philosophers or conceptual gardeners. While I make modest claims to being a gardener, I make none whatever to being a philosopher, which is why, perhaps, I think, I am in sympathy with Pérchère's views. A garden is an assemblage, principally of vegetation, kept in a preferred state of ecological arrest by the craft of gardening: remove the control and it ceases to be a garden.[4] As to its being historic, if in any stage in its growth or decay a garden is judged a work of art, then that can only be a retrospective judgment and that, since chance plays so large a part in a garden's growth, we must agree that the designer is only partly responsible for its success or failure, which is perhaps why Repton wanted to be judged more by his writings than by the gardens he created. The definition which was arrived at by the Fontainebleau delegates stated that: 'An historic garden is an architectural and horticultural composition of interest to the public from the historical and artistic point of view'. And the Garden History Society eventually concluded in 1974 that *An historic garden is a defined area deliberately created as an ornamental environment and of historical interest as such. The term includes designed landscapes.*

THE GARDEN HISTORY SOCIETY

The origins of the Garden History Society are to be found in the *Shell Gardens Book* which was published in 1964 and for which 28 authors contributed short articles on subjects chosen by the editor, Peter Hunt. In the following year Peter Hunt invited many of the contributors to the book to the Royal Horticultural Society where they met other nurserymen, writers, teachers, art historians, gardeners, and scientists. As a result of this meeting the Garden History Society was founded. Mr. Hunt was elected chairman and H. F. Clark president. It had been recognized that neither the Royal Horticultural Society, nor the Institute of Landscape Architects, nor the Society of Architectural Historians dealt exclusively with the history of gardens and gardening and it was felt that a new society would fill this gap.

In 1968 a seminar was held at Stowe on the 'Reclamation and Restoration of Gardens' and in 1973 the Society found its cause and established a Conservation Committee to campaign for increased public awareness in the amenity value of historic gardens and the need to protect them. The campaign to protect historic gardens was well-timed, for a good deal of the preparation towards persuading a Member of Parliament to put forward a Private Member's Bill in Parliament had been achieved by the time European Architectural Heritage Year had been designated.

THE DEVELOPMENT OF LEGISLATION

Representations were made to the United Kingdom Committee for EAHY to include gardens as often having equal importance to their complementary buildings: not only were these representations welcomed, but it was also suggested that it was a good opportunity to include a clause about historical gardens in the proposed new Town and Country Amenities Act. Despite the overtures played by ICOMOS on national listing, difficulties of legal definition were forseen and the alternative of grant-aid was sought to statutory legislation. Mr. Shersby referred to his Bill as a Parliamentary contribution to EAHY and an opportunity to consider the conservation of our heritage, the enhancement of our towns and villages and the maintenance of our historic gardens. As Mavis Batey, Secretary of the Garden History Society has observed, 'the Bill contains the first reference to historical gardens in British legislation, and official recognition of their existence is the first step to their protection.'[5]

Previously, under the provisions of the Historical Buildings and Ancient Monuments Act of 1953, garden buildings such as the temples at Stowe and Stourhead, and even the ponds and cascades at Bramham, had received grant aid. What is important about the new clause is its recognition that historic gardens need not be part of an historic building and may, like Pains Hill in Surrey, merit protection in their own right (Plate 15). The amendment to the 1953 Act enables grants to be made available for the preservation of historic buildings, their contents and adjoining land and adds 'or in the upkeep of a garden or other land which appears to the Secretary of State to be of outstanding historic interest but which is not contiguous or adjacent to a building which appears to him to be of outstanding historic or architectural interest.'[6] While a building may qualify for grant-aid because it is either historic *or* of architectural importance, a garden qualifies only on its being historic. Presumably what is inferred here is the importance of the garden's historic style, that it exemplifies those qualities given by Pérchère to which I referred earlier. (I am told by the secretary of the Historic Buildings Council that applications under Section 12 have been received: to date—May 1975—none have been granted.)

While this legislation has been a considerable achievement, the Town and Country Amenities Act which was passed in 1974, does not meet the fullest hopes of the Garden History Society. Unless an owner is aware that he possesses an historic garden he is not likely to request grant-aid; what is still outside control 'are the landforms, vistas, planting and natural water features, the components of wood, water and ground manipulated into landscape compositions in the eighteenth and nineteenth centuries. It is not in fact the actual garden features (which can be listed) but the total landscape design which stands in jeopardy today.'[7] Some help is offered by Section 4 of the Act which adds to the list of special requirements for planning within conservation areas the need to take the 'setting' of the building into account, which provision the Joint Circular (147/4) discourages from being interpreted too narrowly: 'the "setting" of a building may be limited to the immediate surroundings of the building, but often may include land some distance from it',[8] a brave attempt to legislate the practical results of Pope's injunction to Lord Burlington,

> 'Let not each beauty everywhere be spied,
> Where half the skill is decently to hide.
> He gains all points, who pleasingly confounds,
> Surprises, varies, and conceals the bounds.'

The similarities between British and Japanese garden design have so often been pointed out that it is significant that in Japan, city planning law schedules 'urbanization adjustment zones' and 'scenic beauty preservation zones' as a means to protecting those distant prospects which form so large a part of the garden's design. But the problem would seem almost insoluble, for to use Dr. Appleton's terminology, one man's prospect is another man's refuge.[9] Hence tourist facilities on Mt. Hiei impair the view of that mountain from the Entsu-ji Temple garden which it borrows; or in England where the Hilton Hotel's and Knightsbridge Barracks' gain is the Serpentine's loss.

As the Town and Country Amenities Act stands at present a garden alone cannot be designated as a Conservation Area, but no doubt the recommended Advisory Committees will be to weave a sufficiently complex tissue of connections to suggest it forms part of what is or should be a part of a Conservation Area. As in the case in Staffordshire where Chillington, Alton, Weston, Shugborough and Enville have so been protected by a listing of all the garden buildings and their visual connections with each other, with hedges, significant trees, focal points, woodland and vistas. And since the results did not coincide with Staffordshire's boundaries neighbouring authorities were involved. If this example is in any way typical of the implementation of the Act, then it may be true to say that, 'the Conservation Area may well prove to be the best safeguard for the landscape garden.'[10]

THE PROBLEMS OF 'LISTING' HISTORIC GARDENS

There remains the vexed problem of listing. The Garden History Society argues that a national list of historic gardens is essential in order to draw their owners' attention to what they possess and the public's concern for their protection. But what confidence can we have in such a list? Listed buildings are not by any means safe, for in the first four months of EAHY 750 applications for demolition have already been received. Some architects see listing as a threat to their own creative abilities to do better than their past colleagues[11] and in the case of gardens it is salutary to remember that within forty years London was employed to effect picturesque propriety to Repton's practical corrections of Brown's stylistic pedantry *at the same estate*. There is nothing absolute about 'the genius of the place'.

Earlier in this article the educational and cultural value of gardens was discussed. If then the chief object of listing is to educate—and interest—the public, I suggest that the existing National Garden Scheme, the Gardener's Sunday organization and the National Trust, with a total of about 200 gardens open to the public would be a better method, than the more formal kind of listing adopted for buildings. These organizations already exist and the list is not fixed. Nor are the gardens graded in the apparently arbitrary way of buildings, yet such is the method proposed and already begun by ICOMOS. My own suggestion at Fontainebleau was rather than distinguish between grades 1, 2, and 3 the gardens in each country should be rated for their historic and aesthetic importance: (1) internationally, (2) nationally, (3) regionally, (4) locally.

THE MANAGEMENT OF HISTORIC GARDENS

Very few gardens were designed for the large number of people they now attract.

E

As with so many other forms of conservation, if the capacity of the garden is exceeded it ceases to become a place to enjoy. Worse, it may suggest to managers alterations designed to accommodate and attract even greater numbers of people. In the USSR, where this problem is acute some activities are discouraged, but accommodated elsewhere within a surrounding 'protection zone' in order that the historic garden may be used for walking and sitting only.[12] It may even be necessary—as is the case with the caves at Lascaux—to close the garden altogether. And since it is suggested that some gardens are as internationally important as the Lascaux paintings they must receive proportionate funds and expert attention to conserve them. These are probably few in number, and of financial necessity there can be only few, but the hope is that gardens of international importance would remain in perpetuity. For those in the other categories the funds would be proportionately less, while the number of gardens would be larger. I realize that such a method would decrease the chances of a garden of local importance (grade 4) ever achieving the value of grade 1—not perhaps the least of its short-comings—but my attempt is to put forward a system of dynamic listing which takes account of changing circumstances and judgments in a manner analogous to the dynamism of the garden itself.

But can ICOMOS, the Garden History Society, the Town and Country Amenities Act do much to help the management of historic gardens? Unfortun-ately, the answer is almost certainly no. The chairman of a working party set up by the Country Landowners' Association to look into the problem of garden owners said that 'If the Government cannot be persuaded to act swiftly, half the gardens in the country will be closed in the next 10 years'. Owners of non-commercial gardens cannot offset losses against any other income; the Treasury does not accept historic gardens in lieu of death duties and what the effect of the proposed wealth tax will be no-one knows. And when considering some gardens as unique and irreplaceable works of art there is little doubt that 'the future looks very bleak'.[13] But I have suggested—somewhat to the consternation of some of my Garden History Society friends—that the conservation of gardening is more important than the conservation of gardens; that the justification for historic gardens conservation is that it maintains important skills and examples from which we all can learn.

CONCLUSIONS

When writing about the twentieth century garden Miles Hadfield quoted from the constitution of the British Institute of Landscape Architects, which was founded in 1929, viz. that it set out to correct what was seen as a decline in land-scape and garden design by, among other means, 'the creation and maintenance of a high standard of professional qualification'. Having acknowledged that in-tention Hadfield writes, 'As in the past, however, the talented and experienced amateur, devoting a lifetime to one garden, almost invariably produced some-thing nearer to perfection than the professional who was called in to provide a design, carried it out, and then departed.' Miles Hadfield, gardener and writer about gardens and gardening, is the current President of the Garden History Society and among his many achievements he has devoted a lifetime to making his own garden in Herefordshire.[14] H. F. Clark, the landscape architect and its first President (1966-1971), achieved some part of his professional distinction by writing about his revered early eighteenth century amateur landscape makers and who did not devote very much of his lifetime to making his own garden anywhere. Different though these men are, the Garden History Society sees both to be of Presidential rank, equally able to represent its aims. Let me make it clear that I am not comparing the man Clark with the man Hadfield, what I wish to emphasize is Hadfield's own distinction between the amateur and the professional. George Clarke has written of Stowe, 'Now that garden design has become a reputable branch of art history, it is too readily assumed that every layout must have been designed by a professional. But this was not necessarily the case. Gardening has always been more empirical than the other visual arts and the rule of the patron more personal—characteristics which were strengthened when more 'natural' gardening came into fashion.'[15]

Clarke goes on to suggest that Lord Cobham was the direct designer of his own gardens and that, by the 1740s, Cobham was the most experienced garden designer in the kingdom. The tradition, then, which Hadfield describes is the older and longer; the main highway from which 'professional' excitement is a diversion if not a lay-by. Hence if, in conserving historic gardens, we are conserving the amateur we should treat the professions of art-history or law or landscape architecture or architecture with some caution. And let it be said that the Garden History Society is not a professional institute, that two of the most important gardens in Britain were made in the way Hadfield described (Stowe and Stourhead) and that they are also the two gardens about which we know most, thanks to George Clarke and Kenneth Woodbridge[16] devoting a large part of their lifetime to their study and conservation.

Of garden restoration H. F. Clark has written, 'I imagine that the restorer should avoid a too pedantic approach to period accuracy, especially in planting. What I should imagine to be more important is scale and understanding of the original designer's intentions.[17] Which is much more easily done when the designer is a professional and the restorer can depend upon plans, reports and documents etc. It is when the designer is an amateur in the Hadfield sense that, unless there are men like Clarke and Woodbridge, the restorer is dependent upon so much guesswork that the result is too often a pastiche of the style. It is in this sense that garden—and landscape—conservation differs from other kinds of conservation. It is the activity resulting in a garden or landscape which conserves soil, plants and animals. And as I have already suggested it is the activity which needs conserving quite as much as its most revered expression.

NOTES AND REFERENCES

1 Balchin, W. G. V., *Cornwall, an illustrated essay on the history of the landscape.* (see also W. G. Hoskin's introduction pp. xi, xii), London, 1954, p. 15.

2 Sylvia Crowe puts Gertrude Jekyll's garden into the context of garden design in Crowe, Sylvia, *Garden Design*, London, 1968.

3 ICOMOS, *Proceedings of the First International Symposium on the Protection and Restoration of Historical Gardens*, Davis, 1971.

4 Fricker, Laurence J., *Special Problems Connected with the conservation of gardens of historical interest in Great Britain*, Report to the Symposium organized by ICOMOS and IFLA (See Note 3, p. 2).

5 Batey, Mavis, *Grant Aid for Historic Gardens*, paper read at the Edinburgh University symposium on Historic Garden Conservation, December 1974. My thanks to Mrs. Batey, the Secretary of the Garden History Society, to quote from her paper before proceedings of the Symposium are published.

6 *Town & Country Planning Amenities Act 1974*, section 12.

7 Batey, Mavis, op. cit.

8 *Circular 147/74*, Department of Environment; *Circular 220/74*, Welsh office, para. 23.

9 Appleton, Jay, *The Experience of Landscape*, London, 1975.

10 Batey, Mavis, op. cit.

11 Thompson, M., 'The Architect's Dilemma' to be published in *Architectural Design* (expected 1975). My thanks to Mr. Thompson for allowing me to quote from his article which is in preparation.

12 *ICOMOS* Proceedings, 1970, p. 165.

13 Robinson, Anne, 'How long will the money flow in our English country gardens?', *Sunday Times*, August 18, 1974.

14 Hadfield, Miles, *Gardening in Britain*, London, 1960, p. 429.

15 Clarke, George, 'Heresy in Stowe's Elysium' (in) *Furor Hortensis; essays in the history of the English Landscape Garden in memory of H. F. Clark*, Edited Willis, Edinburgh, 1974, p. 52. See also 'The Gardens of Stowe' and 'Grecian taste and Gothic Virtue', *Apollo*, June 1973.

16 Woodbridge, Kenneth, *Landscape and Antiquity, aspects of English Culture at Stourhead 1718–1838*, 1970, and Woodbridge, Kenneth, *The Stourhead Landscape*, National Trust, 1971.

17 *Garden History Society occasional paper No. 1*, 1969.

Norwich

A fine old city

GERALD DIX

'Norwich has everything—a cathedral, a major castle on a mound right in the middle, walls and towers, an undisturbed medieval centre with winding streets and alleys, thirty-two medieval parish churches and a river'.[1] In its City Hall it has possibly 'the foremost English public building of between the wars',[2] recent architecture and planning of unusual sensitivity and a civic society that can justifiably be proud of its achievement over more than half a century. It had, so Pevsner wrote in 1961,[3] a prouder sense of civic responsibility than any other town of its size in Britain; those who love Norwich, which must be a higher proportion of those who know it than is the case in almost any other town in this country, will agree that this is still so.

HISTORICAL DEVELOPMENT

At the time of the conquest, when Norwich had a population of 5 500, it ranked third amongst British cities, being exceeded in size only by London and York. Construction of the Cathedral began in 1096:[4] it was at that time that the castle was first built on its great mound, only to be reconstructed in the middle of the twelfth century more or less in the form we know today. The city walls, replacing a ditch and bank, were begun towards the end of the thirteenth century and were completed in 1343, 'over 2 miles long, 20 feet high and 5 feet thick, with towers at intervals and gates where the main thoroughfares crossed'.[5] Despite the Black Death, which in 1349 caused the deaths of almost one third of the population, trade in the city grew rapidly in the fourteenth century, when there was an influx of immigrants from Europe. The city received its first charter towards the end of the twelfth century[6] and by a later charter in 1404, was granted authority to elect a mayor, sherriffs and aldermen. The street pattern, surviving houses and rich treasury of churches, provide ample testimony of the prosperity of the city between the fourteenth and sixteenth centuries.

In the middle ages the wealth of Norwich, as indeed of most of Norfolk, was firmly based on the woollen trade. Even as late as 1723 Defoe's comments indicated that the city's prosperity was still essentially based on weaving and cloth.[7] As the native skills and trade declined, foreign workers were encouraged to settle in Norwich, bringing new skills and a love both of gardening and of canary breeding.[8] In 1586 the city was granted a charter enlarging its area to approximately 3 238 hectares,[9] an area retained with but little change until after the second World War. Subsequently, the growth of industries associated with an expanding agricultural technology and a wider range of products increased the prosperity of Norwich and its importance as a regional centre. Later industrial developments included leather working and brewing and, from the middle of the eighteenth century, banking and insurance. By the middle of the nineteenth century the cloth trade had declined, but new industries included chocolate and cocoa making, the manufacture of mustard and starch. Leather working had led to the establishment of the boot and shoe industry. More recently, electrical engineering, the manufacture of ironwork and wire netting machinery, timber milling, briefly also of aircraft production, gave Norwich a broad economic base to cushion the city against the worst effects of depression.[10] During all of this time the city continued to grow from 5 000 in the late fourteenth century to 15 000 a hundred years later, just under 30 000 by 1700, 40 000 by 1800, more than doubling by 1900 and reaching 120 000 by 1921. The population has remained at about this figure since that time, growth over the last half century being in the outer areas, beyond the city limits. The population within the new Norwich District boundary—more or less the built up area of Greater Norwich—is estimated to be 223 000 (1971)[11] and is expected to grow by about 50 000 in the next twenty years.

Recently published employment figures[12] indicate a high demand for labour in Norwich where 54 per cent of 1969 employment was in service industries, 34 per cent in manufacturing, eight per cent in building and four per cent in primary industry. A decline in the shoe making and leather trades has been more than matched by an increase in engineering and electrical manufacturing and other recent growth areas have included retailing, insurance, chemicals and food and drink manufacturing. Although most of the growth has arisen from the expansion of existing local establishments two major introductions have been the University of East Anglia and the transfer to Norwich of part of Her Majesty's Stationery Office. A significant increase in shopping and office employment in the central area, has to some extent been counterbalanced by the transfer of some manufacturing industries and employment associated with the cattle market to out-of-centre sites.

THE NORWICH MARKETS

Norwich for many years had three, later two, major market areas. Tombland, an open space since Saxon times, was for long the site of 'temporary' market stalls. It also accommodated the fair that nowadays causes chaos through its twice yearly occupation of the old cattle market site at peak shopping and holiday times. Tombland today serves as a car park and link between the city and the cathedral close, its glory gone but its buildings fortunately mostly retained, even though their use has changed.

The cattle market has been transferred almost three kilometres down the Ipswich Road from its former location on a high and prominent site adjoining the castle. The removal can only have been advantageous for the city as well as for the traders, but it has left a void that is inadequately even if conveniently filled by its use as a car park. In such a location something more appropriate is surely called for.

The Norwich market place itself is large, bustling and the site of buildings of character and in many cases of quality also. On its western side the market place, and indeed the whole of the central area, is dominated by the City Hall of

1923-38. Designed by C. H. James and Rowland Pierce, built of Ketton stone and grey brown bricks in the Scandinavian manner beloved of the near modern architects of the period this polygonally pillared building with its 60 metre tower has been absorbed, or perhaps one should say, accepted, as part of the urban scene. It displays a quality and care of detailing lacking in many buildings of more recent date. The provision market, at its feet, really does function as a market should, supplying a wide range of foods to citizens of all classes from Norwich and the surrounding areas.

TRAFFIC

Although Norwich is not on the pilgrimage map, being fifty miles east of the tourist lane from London to Ely and Cambridge, Peterborough and Lincoln,[13] it is on the main motor route for many holiday makers bound for Yarmouth and the Norfolk Coast. This traffic affects Norwich in two ways. First, at weekends and on bank holidays in the summer season there is a significant amount of by-passable traffic for which up to the present no proper provision has been made.[14] Secondly, in times of inclement weather holiday makers from the coast and the Norfolk Broads converge on the city centre for entertainment and shopping. This places considerable strain on the not ungenerous car parking facilities, and on the basically medieval street pattern that persists to the present day. The street pattern 'was tied up interfaced in knots centuries ago, and it has never been unwound'.[15] Any attempt at urban conservation must be dependent on the removal of as much through traffic as possible, and thus ultimately on the construction of a southern by-pass. The predominantly radial form of major roads in the Norwich area was the subject of one of the studies included in the Buchanan report 'Traffic in Towns' in 1963[16] and this has undoubtedly influenced latter day thinking on transportation planning in the city.

Cathedral, Churches and City Character

Norwich, in John Betjeman's words, 'wears its cathedral like a crown, a coronal of flying buttresses, supporting the walls of glass. The stone was brought over the sea from France to build and adorn the cathedral church of the Holy and Undivided Trinity'.[17] The Cathedral Close is approached by two great gates opening on to Tombland, and through the lower close by Pull's Ferry. St. Ethelbert's, the southerly of the two gates was built in 1316, heavily restored by Wilkins[18] and sensitively and recently by Bernard Feilden. Erpingham Gate, 1420, leads directly to the recently restored but somewhat disappointing West Front of the Cathedral, a relationship which has provided Feilden with the opportunity to introduce some new perspectively-patterned paving and cobbles which integrate floor and wall surfaces into a single composition and by texture and colour link the Cathedral through the Close with Tombland beyond. The Close, almost a village in itself, admirably maintained and estate-managed, clusters round a Cathedral which is distinguished most perhaps by its crocketed spire, the second highest in England, and one of the three major landmarks in the town. Because of the size of the close in which it stands and because of its form, the Cathedral, long and low apart from the spire and the gates to Tombland, makes much less general impact on the townscape than one might expect, and less possibly than Gilbert Scott's Church of St. John the Baptist of 1884–1910, which is to be consecrated as a Cathedral in the Roman Catholic Church.

Norwich has many other churches. 'Round the corner, down the steps, over the bridge, up the hill, there's always a church: grandest of all, St. Peter Mancroft—so large that sometimes people mistake it for the cathedral'.[19] Not all the churches are now used for religious purposes—St. Peter Hungate is a museum, St. Edmund Fishergate is a store, St. Simon and St. Jude a Boy Scout headquarters, but they all play their part in preserving the character of the town, linking present activities with past history. Most Norwich churches are flint, or predominantly flint, sometimes knapped, materials giving them a character of their own, linking them in scale and texture with other wall and floor surfaces on secular buildings.

The character of the city owes much to topography, to the winding route followed by the Rivers Wensum and Yare and to the retention of a major part of the medieval pattern of streets. In its early days Norwich evidently kept a more strict control over trade guilds and their activities than was the case elsewhere.[20] In the absence of any nearby coal field and the consequential absence of any large scale growth during the Industrial Revolution, many buildings remain from Georgian times and there are good examples of medieval Elizabethan and Jacobean buildings. The general scale, form and texture of most secular buildings before the beginning of this century is domestic; and among them rendered colour washed walls, brickwork, some of very good quality, and tile roof predominate. There are of course a number of larger buildings, but they are neither so many or so concentrated as to dominate and many are now under pressure for replacement. In Botolph Street, in 1903, A. F. Scott built a clothing factory which was a plain, straightforward industrial building, following the tradition of John Brown's yarn mill of 1834, now Jarrold's works. Both use new and old materials but both, the former by its size and the latter by elements in its design, are related to traditional domestic forms: though both impress, neither dominates. Until very recent years most other large buildings, or larger than domestic scale buildings, have been so located as not to obtrude into the townscape, so that one was unaware of their size unless they were carefully examined, or unless they have had something definite and acceptable to contribute to the street scene. Barclay's Bank on Bank Plain,[21] a one and a quarter life sized (almost) Renaissance Palace that is not any too big for its site or surroundings, is an example of the former while the National Westminster Bank, London Street,[22] exemplifies the second category. It is only fifty years old but might have been there for a century longer, is simple but has character, scale and materials satisfactorily to fulfill an important visual role in an important city street. Skipper's Norwich Union Insurance Offices, 1903-4, all recesses and rustication, sit a little pompously in Surrey Street, but they have conviction, add much to the street scene and are not inconsiderate to their neighbours. The much bigger and very recent Eastern Daily Press building adjoining the old cattle market displays the same qualities

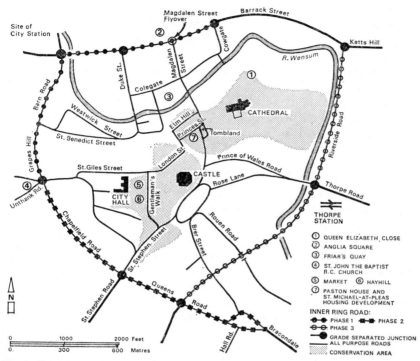

Fig. 1 Diagrammatic plan of central Norwich, showing the location of principal landmarks and planning proposals. It is not expected, in view of the current economic situation, that the third stage of the inner ring road will be built in the foreseeable future

of seemliness and 'fit' to its site and surroundings. There are two other features that have helped to do much for the character of Norwich in the past and which form the basis of possible patterns for conservation and future redevelopment. These are the yards and courts and the pedestrian streets.

Yards and courts were common in Norwich from Elizabethan and Jacobean times when the workers in the cloth and leather trades began to occupy the surrounding small overcrowded dwellings. At the turn of the last century there were 749 yards and courts in Norwich and even in the 1970s more than a hundred remain within the area of the old walled city.[23] Once overcrowded, undrained and frequently ill maintained, they now provide an opportunity for conservation and improvement of conveniently located small size environmental areas; an inducement not for cellular renewal but rather for unitary upgrading.[24]

Norwich has recently become well known for its policy of pedestrianization, but it can be argued that this is not a new idea but the continuation of a tradition. Some of the narrow lanes off London Street have been free of traffic for very many years, and at least a part of Davey Place which runs between Castle Meadow and the Market Place, (strictly, Gentleman's Walk) and provides a visual link between the castle keep and the City Hall has evidently been a pedestrian way since it was constructed in 1812.[25] The Royal Arcade, by Skipper, parallel with

Davey Place, unadorned to the Market Place 'but very naughty once its back is turned'[26] merely continued in an amusing Art Nouveau manner a Norwich tradition for providing conveniently and with regard for the rest of the city, what its citizens require.

The character of the centre of Norwich may be summarized as being predominantly modest in scale and size, the generally and well kept and simply proportioned buildings pleasantly related one to another, with here and there, but perhaps recently too frequently, some not altogether successful importations in the commercial international style.

Some Major Pre-war Developments

Without doubt, the biggest single piece of development to be carried out in the centre of Norwich in the years before the war was the building of the new City Hall. In addition to providing a major new land-mark and better working conditions than those in the rat-infested offices that it replaced,[27] the City Hall scheme involved the expansion and embellishment of the old provision market. Further, the street pattern in the heart of the city was changed, narrow roads being straightened, widened and generally improved to make them more suitable for motor traffic. (See Fig. 1 for the locations of principal landmarks).

There had been earlier modifications to the old town layout to take account of the needs of traffic. Although the railways had found it impossible to penetrate to the central area, their stations were built within a reasonably short distance. Thorpe Station, 1844, the lone survivor, one and a quarter kilometres east of the castle and immediately adjoining the River Wensum was linked to the centre by Prince of Wales Road, 1860, a wide road with trees down the middle, imperiously cutting a great swathe across an older street pattern of a smaller scale. Because of its shape and its mature trees Prince of Wales road is now more attractive and visually more important as an ensemble than the sum of its parts would suggest. At the city end of the road the view drifts away, being only partly closed by the terra cotta colour of the Royal Hotel, a building reminiscent of Waterhouse with too much water.

In the later years of the nineteenth century and the earlier ones of the twentieth, there were other changes in the road pattern, mainly to meet the needs of the electric tramways that appeared, only to vanish from the scene within 35 years. Some of these developments involved street widening like that along Castle Meadow on the west side of the castle mound, or the punching through older property of short lengths of acceptable gradient and radius, as between Castle Meadow and Red Lion Street at the expense of the Bell Hotel, and between Redwell Street and St. Andrews.[28] At a later date the widening of St. Stephens, the main approach from London, was considered but it was not carried out until some years after the war. In the immediate pre-war period a number of new buildings were set back to allow for road widening in various parts of the city: the consequent short lengths of wide road, resembling unexpected parking bays, are to this day affectionately but irreverently known to the *cognoscenti* by the name of the engineer of the time.

City Pride and Citizen Endeavour

The development of the market area, the various road proposals—however misguided, with the advantages of hindsight, we may consider them—slum clearance and housing programmes pointed to the emergence and development of civic pride, and in Norwich citizens and council had a city of which at least some realized they could justifiably be proud. Writing in 1927, H. V. Morton said that 'there comes a time in the life of old cities where the City Fathers should form a coalition Government to decide whether their city is to preserve its ancient beauty or to become a second Leicester or a little Birmingham. Norwich, it seems to me, has reached this point ... the local authorities should spend a weekend in Shrewsbury in order to realize the chance that lies immediately before them'.[29] Evidently unknown to him moves had already been taken that have achieved much that Mr. Morton hoped for, without the need to follow his suggestion that the architects of Georgian banks be imprisoned in the eminently suitable castle dungeons.

THE NORWICH SOCIETY

In 1923 the Norwich Society had been founded by a group of citizens who were concerned at the lack of official recognition of the environmental quality of the city. Their aim was not to prevent new developments, which they have always seen as being essential to Norwich's role as a regional capital, but to ensure that the many buildings which give the city its character were carefully examined before redevelopment, in order to make sure that nothing of value was destroyed.[30] If conservation is defined as the wise use of resources their policy was, and remains, one of alert and imaginative conservation rather than sterile preservation.

The Norwich Society had its first major success in 1927, the very year when H. V. Morton was calling for action. Elm Hill 'is the most picturesque street in Norwich. There is not a single house ... which could be disturbing'.[31] At that time it was derelict and threatened with demolition. It remains because of the diligence of the founder members of the Norwich Society and through the courage of the Mayor who gave his casting vote for its saving. It has since become a centre for art and antique dealers, and for many of the arts and crafts shops that have proliferated in recent years. More recently it has apparently been saved from excessive traffic loading by the adoption of a scheme prepared in his private capacity by a police officer.[32] (See Plate 18).

The Norwich Society has had many other successes and some disappointments during the years through which it has maintained a vigilant eye on many planning matters in the city. The city fathers should be grateful that in the Norwich Society there is a responsible body concerned with the city as a whole and not with any one area or aspect of planning. It is, therefore, able to present a more balanced view commanding a wider measure of support than might otherwise be the case. There must be many city officers who have been glad to have the enlightened support of the Norwich Society over the years, and who have been perhaps not altogether unfearful of its censure, in their task of furthering the proper development of the urban environment.

Some Planning Proposals

Despite its new City Hall and emergent civic pride, before the last war Norwich lacked a comprehensive development plan, although a scheme for the built up area of the town was in course of preparation in 1939.[33] Following air raids on the city, C. H. James, ARA and S. Rowland Pierce, the architects of the City Hall, were appointed to prepare a plan for the city in co-operation with H. C. Rowley, City Engineer. Their report was published in 1945, with the intention that it should form the basis for the growth and development of Norwich during the ensuing fifty years, there being room within its broad design for flexibility and for the exercise of discretion in its execution.[34]

The central area, basically that of the medieval town, was to be divided into a number of precincts separated from one another by major roads. The precinct principle, some bold road proposals and a number of design and land use recommendations were the main features of the plan. About many of the ideas there can have been little argument, but about the specific schemes agreement was unlikely even in the period of post-war euphoria. The City Engineer found himself unable to subscribe to the views of his two colleagues about the road plan.

A ring road would require the demolition of those houses that used the city wall as part of the structure of the dwellings, and this was a clear point in favour of the proposal: the houses were in any case largely out of date. The authors of the plan appreciated the need to relieve traffic pressure on Magdalen Street, then the most dangerous street in the city, and were sensitive to its architectural merit, which they regarded as being of importance to the general character of Norwich.[35] They proposed that the ring road should pass to the north of Magdalen Street, thus avoiding the destruction of any property there. Magdalen Street itself would be closed to all vehicular traffic to allow it to remain as a shopping precinct. James and Pierce regarded this as the only alternative to the destruction and consequent loss of one of the most typical of the older streets.[36]

Elsewhere, there were road proposals that would be less readily acceptable today than they might have been thirty years ago. St. Stephens was to be widened to become a dual carriageway entry to the city, with strict design control of fronting buildings. City traffic would be given a choice of routes, the two main ones being along Castle Meadow, between the Castle and shops, or along Gentleman's Walk past the edge of the market which would thereby be separated from most of the major shopping area.

It can be argued that these proposals might not have been unacceptable for the traffic volumes then contemplated, and which are probably less than the 'unimproved' streets cope with nowadays. It can also be argued that they are to be preferred to the City Engineer's counter proposal which would have carved dual carriageways not only along the line of St. Stephens, but also northwards past the market (he wanted to move the market itself) to the inner ring road. A further road along the line of Magdalen Street would involve the destruction of the buildings on one side of that street. In an endeavour better to serve the needs of the business community the inner ring road would follow a line further south than James and Pierce had proposed and would cut across Magdalen Street.[37]

Some years later Norwich was selected for one of the case studies in the Buchanan report, *Traffic in Towns*,[38] where problems of planning for a small area containing 400 buildings or groups of buildings listed under the Planning Acts attracted the Minister of Transport's Working Group. The report commented upon the way in which the unity of the town centre was severed by heavy traffic cross flows,[39] several of which converge on Magdalen Street. London Street also suffered from heavy traffic, but the evidence of other streets indicated that road widening alone would not answer the traffic problem but might alter the character of the place. The Buchanan team divided the area into nine self-contained precincts independently connected to a primary road network.[40] Through traffic, including that crossing the river, would be prohibited, except possibly for buses. Magdalen Street would not necessarily be a pedestrian way but would have normal local traffic. Gentleman's Walk and London Street, far from remaining busy streets, were suggested for pedestrianization. The Buchanan team emphasized that their ideas were intended only as a basis for study and discussion and were in no sense a plan; further they dealt only with the inner city.

In 1966 the City Planning Department assumed responsibility for transportation as well as for town planning and the way was open for the production of an integrated scheme for the future of Norwich. The aim of the urban plan was to develop Norwich further as a regional centre, to preserve the character of the historic city, to evolve a location policy for population increase in the city area and to cater for overspill from London.[41] In the centre it was intended to have a traffic free core, to conserve the Cathedral area, consolidate those parts threatened by the motor car invasion, encourage change in outworn areas and encourage residential development in the city centre.[42]

These prudent objectives advanced by the City Planning Officer, were to be achieved by a plan based on a ring and loop road system. As in the James and Pierce plan of 1945, a ring would more or less follow the line of the old city walls and from it loops would enter the central area. From each loop there would be routes for servicing and access to premises and for car parking. Through traffic, other than buses, would be prohibited and there would be two major pedestrian areas, each largely coincidental with major conservation areas. A southern by-pass was an essential feature of the plan as was the encouragement of the growth of shopping centres within environmental areas round the centre. The line of the inner ring road was to be safeguarded as were the locations for the loop roads that would serve the area within the ring.[43] These measures were to be taken in the interests not just of the environment and central area conservation but also in an endeavour to enhance the quality of urban life.

It will be evident that whilst all the major contributors to the planning debate in Norwich have emphasized the architectural merit of the city, widely different emphasis has been given to environmental quality in the exposition of planning proposals. This has been especially the case in the reconciliation of the conflict between pressures for the retention of existing buildings and those to cater for the anticipated volume of vehicular traffic in years to come, pressures which are greatest of all in historic towns and cities.

Traffic Policy and Road Construction

'There is no one easy and complete solution to the problem posed by the growth of motor traffic', each remedy, each line of approach reacting immediately on all of the others.[44] Clearly in the case of Norwich whatever solution there may be for the traffic problem, and thus to a considerable extent to the challenge to improve the quality of the environment, must be found outside the city core. There are great difficulties in road building anywhere, but in the heart of an ancient city and especially one of the quality of Norwich they are immense. For a long time it has been apparent that traffic pressure in Norwich can only be eased by the improvement of roads in the outer areas, and in particular by the construction of a major route by-passing the city.

The James-Pierce-Rowley plan included proposals[45] for an outer ring road swinging round the north of the city on a radius of about three to three and a half kilometres from the castle. This road was intended primarily to carry holiday traffic to the Norfolk Broads and Yarmouth, but one may question the wisdom of suggesting a road so far away from the centre and taking such a long route round the city. At an average distance of over a kilometre within the by-pass, an intermediate distributor road would carry traffic of a more local character. Inside this, and immediately surrounding the city walls, was to be the Inner Ring Road. This inner road proposal was not entirely new, for in 1936 the City Council had considered proposals for a partial ring, then incomplete on the southern side—the side used by most coast bound traffic—and rather too close in in relation to Magdalen Street.

The problem of the southern section crossing the deep and fairly wide valley of the Wensum—Norwich not being as topographically simple as many may suppose—was to be solved by the construction of a viaduct above the river.[46] The object was to facilitate uninterrupted traffic flow round the town centre. The City Engineer thought that the ring was too widely drawn and that traffic would continue to pass through the town to the detriment of its environment and character. Instead of a viaduct he proposed an inner ring road descending through a tunnel down to river level where it would cross by swing bridge. Would not the possibility of delay on this fairly direct line have caused traffic to travel instead through the city centre?

In the end, the southern section of the inner ring was never built and the northern part slices through Magdalen Street, more or less as the City Engineer proposed. The traffic situation has deteriorated and its volume has increased. In the interests of the conservation and of the character of the city a new and complete system to remove remaining traffic from the centre is urgently needed. Proposals have now been prepared by the Department of the Environment for a southern by-pass[47] and these must be considered in conjunction with the inner ring and other proposals of the Norwich Area Transportation Study's Strategy for 1986,[48] which examines the pros and cons of alternative strategies. In each case the objectives are the same and relate mobility and accessibility with the needs of conservation in a city which should be zealously guarded as part of the nation's heritage.[49]

In this study we see the clearest statement of the relationship between the positive aspects of development, including road building and traffic management. The Norfolk Joint Structure Plan reports[50] emphasize these links and relate conservation policies to alternative forms of layout that might be adopted should greater Norwich continue to grow at the rate considered reasonable two years or so ago.

Some of the recent proposals are likely to be more expensive than the local authorities can afford. Central government will only contribute to road construction forming part of the national network. If it is accepted that, environmentally, Norwich is of national importance, that it is an important part of the British heritage and not just of that of East Anglia, is there not a case for national support for measures to conserve and indeed to enhance its environmental quality? The argument for support of this kind was expressed by Sir Patrick and Lascelles Abercrombie in their report on Stratford-upon-Avon published more than fifty years ago,[51] and again in the draft Urban Plan for Norwich.[52] It reappears now in relation to the proper consideration of the relationship between transportation and architecture, a matter which involves decisions about the wise use of resources.

Development and Conservation: Successes and Disappointments

The success and eventual far-sightedness of the Norwich Society and the Norwich City Council in the preservation of Elm Hill has already been noted. A further considerable success came in 1959 with the completion by the Civic Trust in co-operation with the Norwich Society, of the face-lift scheme for Magdalen Street. The project may be criticized for its superficiality, for concentrating only on appearance and for its failure to deal with the major planning issues related to the prosperity of that part of the city. Such criticisms may be justified, but they relate to considerations outside the scope of the project. The intention was to show that with thought and care, above all with goodwill and co-operation between all interested parties, the environment *could* easily be improved. Co-ordinated colour schemes, the clearing away of clutter and the elimination of unnecessary signs helped immeasurably to integrate the diverse parts of the street picture. The influence of the Magdalen Street scheme was considerable and it was emulated in many other towns. In Norwich it was undoubtedly a factor in persuading property owners in other parts of the city that there were merits in co-ordinated improvement, in the wise husbandry of the built environment.

The success of the Civic Trust scheme was followed by disappointment in relation to another aspect of development in the same area.

Following a public inquiry, the City Engineer's recommended line of the Inner Ring Road was confirmed, cutting through, or passing over, Magdalen Street at Stump Cross, significantly reducing the length of Magdalen Street worthy of conservation. Although the new ring road is undoubtedly advantageous from the traffic point of view it constitutes a visual watershed in a precious area of townscape, one side being characteristically Norwich, the other almost anywhere. The Stationery Office Building, inspired perhaps—but inadequately so—

by the Gowan architecture of Cambridge and Leicester, and the adjoining Anglia Square (See Plate 19) are in a part of the city where they have minimal effect on the skyline, yet are not too inconvenient for the user. And, certainly, the relationship of ring road, car parking, shopping piazza and cinema has much to commend it. Anglia Square itself is a little hard and often windswept; by its very size it lacks the intimacy of the rest of Norwich's shopping area and the materials used are those that will minimize weathering and the collection of the patina of age. A location a hundred metres or so further north would have been preferable.

After Magdalen Street, the next major development in Norwich's planning progress was the pedestrianization of London Street. An appraisal of central area streets had drawn attention to the danger to pedestrians and vehicles in a busy street with a five-metre carriageway and inadequate pavements, carrying heavy peak hour traffic flows. Studies were made to benefit from experience in Copenhagen, Essen, Dusseldorf and Cologne[53] before the Norwich proposal was put forward. London Street contains a wide variety of shops, the majority providing high class specialist services. Fumes and considerable noise were caused by traffic flows which, on summer weekdays, exceeded 3 000 vehicles per day in each direction. Clearly, merely to close London Street would only exacerbate the traffic situation elsewhere and a number of related proposals were considered.[54]

After considerable discussion within the corporation and with interested outside bodies, including the Norwich Society and the London Street Traders Association, an experimental scheme was operated for three months in the summer of 1967.[55] Pedestrian use of the street increased, the shoppers and subsequently, the shop-keepers, later confirming their approval of the scheme. Twenty-eight of the thirty-two shops on London Street reported increased trade. The effect on motorists' journey times was found to be negligible. In the light of these circumstances it is hardly surprising that a permanent scheme quickly followed, incorporating lessons learnt in the experiment (See Plate 16).

London Street, like Magdalen Street, comprises a series of buildings of varied architectural merit and some of no merit whatsoever, which together form an interesting street picture. The curve of the street, with its closed views down side streets and footways and at one end terminated by the distant Cathedral Spire, at the other by the Guildhall and the City Hall Spire, give it a quality that is uncommon in a major urban shopping street. It is a pattern which owes everything to its gradual evolution rather than to consciously applied principles of civic design. It is important that the same evolutionary process should continue.

One may assess recent developments with mixed feelings. In 1970 one of the larger elements in the street picture, a store and restaurant, was so badly damaged by fire that it had to be demolished. Its replacement is no doubt a much more manageable building. In plan outline it is strikingly similar to its predecessor, but it is a little taller, much smoother, with a large area of a single texture lacking the interest given to the old shop by its pilasters: above all it lacks points of reference to the human scale. The design exercise was undertaken by the developer's architects in co-operation with the local planning officers. At some point a compromise is necessary; in this case one feels that, whilst the general framework is appropriate, the detail is disappointing. How much control can, or should, a planning office exercise?

The same question may be asked in relation to the redevelopment of Hay Hill where 'an unashamed Georgian warehouse, four storeys, eleven bays long and completely plain'[56] has been replaced at the end of its useful life by a shop of generally similar bulk. Except for the ground floor the new building is largely windowless, and amply demonstrates the difference between 'size' and 'scale' in architecture. On such a prominent site, cheek by jowl with St. Peter Mancroft in its splendid position above the market place, the Norfolk Parish Church *par excellence*,[57] and adjoining a public house and shops of modest but pleasant proportions, one could have hoped for more loving care to be devoted to the detail of this new element in the townscape—or was it too consciously considered, too carefully related to the rules so that it lacks the sparkle of spontaneity in design? At least the redevelopment provided the opportunity for the removal of some barbarously pruned trees (over the dead body, so to say, of the Norwich Society and many others besides), a moth-eaten looking patch of grass and some redundant roadway. They have been replaced by a pleasantly designed piece of hard landscape and water. There is a lot that is more disappointing in Norwich then the Hay Hill development, but in a city of high quality one assesses these matters against higher standards than is the case in lesser places. On balance one may perhaps regard the result as a goal-less draw.

An area with almost unlimited potential and problems for the future is the old cattle market site, on a ridge adjoining the castle. A decade or so ago there was a considerable area hereabouts that might well have been redeveloped for the University of East Anglia, then seeking a site. What a golden opportunity to build an urban university, not merely *in* the town, but *of* the town. In that location it could have contributed so much more, culturally and visually, than is now possible from its more remote Earlham site, however imaginatively that may be developed. Critics of the idea said that the town site, stretching south between Ber Street and King Street to Bracondale where the new County Hall now sticks up on the skyline like a sore thumb, would have been too congested or too expensive or would have generated too much traffic. Certainly it would have posed problems. Some new uses, and some new buildings such as the wholly admirable Eastern Daily Press offices, would have to have been located elsewhere, as would at least one of the City Architect's eminently satisfactory housing schemes. The arguments against the urban university prevailed and the opportunity has passed. The city now has its peripheral campus with Lasdun's imaginative ziggurats and Feilden and Mawson's sympathetic alliance with the landscape. In the interests of urbanity and conservation, the rejection of the town site is to be regretted. Care must be taken to see that no similar chances are missed in the future.

The Architectural Heritage and Heritage Year

Norwich's architectural standards are high, as examples of its civic awareness have demonstrated. Recent schemes, including those for European Architectural

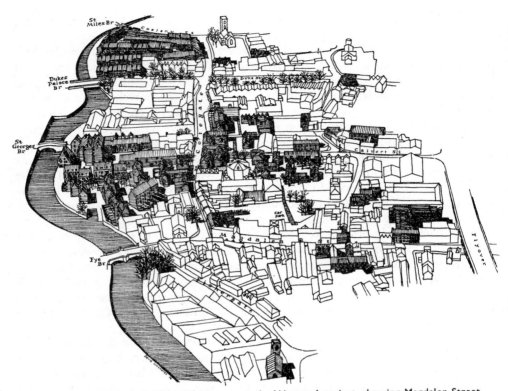

Fig. 2 Drawing of the area of the 'Heritage over the Wensum' project, showing Magdalen Street running from Fye Bridge to the flyover of the inner ring road. The Friar's Quay housing site faces the river between Fye Bridge and St. George's Bridge. The Octagon Chapel, facing Colegate, can be seen in the centre of the drawing. The shaded buildings are where improvements were projected in association with EAHY. This project involved building restoration, the opening up of the riverside, the removal of eyesores and the development of new infill. The impressive results so far achieved resulted in the scheme being chosen as one of sixteen of exceptional merit in the list of 285 projects which received Heritage Year Awards from the Civic Trust. Each of the sixteen schemes received a bronze medallion donated by the Goldsmith's Company as its contribution to European Architectural Heritage Year

Heritage Year, will surely further enhance the reputation of its architects, just as they improve the fabric of the town.

Enfolded in a wall of the Cathedral Close the observant visitor will find Queen Elizabeth Close, a most sensitive piece of domestic architecture, by Simon Crosse of the Feilden and Mawson office. The scale is right, the materials appropriate, especially where old and new abut, and the whole scheme including brick-patterned paving, forms a single composition. The price, too, was right, for these dwellings for elderly people were built at yardstick costs, with additions only for double glazing.

Across the river and south of the Magdalen Street flyover on the inner ring road is the site of 'Heritage over the Wensum,' the specific contribution that Norwich is making to EAHY (see Fig. 2 above and Plate 20). The organization established for the EAHY programme brings together trade and professional[58] associations, developers, the Norwich Society and the City Council. Many buildings in the area are individually of considerable architectural merit and historic interest: together they form an area of outstanding townscape quality.

Running east-west through the middle of the site and parallel with the River Wensum is Colegate, which not only has some of the best early houses in the city but also the Congregational Old Meeting, a hipped roof, red brick building of 1693 which is being repaired and modified for supplementary use as a music centre. Nearby is Thomas Ivory's elegant Octagon Chapel of 1754-6, built for the Presbyterians and only later becoming Unitarian. A few metres further along the street is St. George's Church, the surroundings of which are being tidied up.

Most of the land behind the Colegate Street frontage and the river was for many years the site of a timber yard and a glassworks. The glassworks is now the subject of a face lift scheme promoted by the owner and an investment firm. The timber yard moved to an out-of-town site a few years ago, leaving an area of about a hectare available for redevelopment in a prime location. The City Council acquired the site and this provided the opportunity to introduce some new central area housing in partnership with a development company. Friar's Quay redevelopment is now almost complete, and very satisfactory it looks too. The architects (Feilden and Mawson again; David Luckhurst, partner in charge) have devised a layout full of excitement and interest, with carefully contrived enclosures of space, some cleverly framed views to and across the river and others that one feels might have just happened, the Gods being kind. The design capacity is 249 bed spaces, at a density of 282 bed spaces per hectare. Buildings and private open space occupy 45 per cent of the ground area.[59] Dwellings are of a variety of sizes, some incorporating garage accommodation, some using communal garage blocks. The river frontage is a public footpath and a feature of the scheme is a launching ramp for small boats—the garages in many houses being large enough for both a car and a boat. The wall materials, french bricks, and the steeply pitched pantile roofs are already weathering well and no doubt after a year or two the development will be regarded as an essential part of the Norwich scene, separated only by the River from the old world of Elm Hill and but short distance from the city centre, Magdalen Street and Anglia Square (See Plate 20).

In other parts of the Wensum area restoration work is being carried out in partnership by the Norwich Preservation Trust Limited and the City Council.[60] In Magdalen Street the frontages of one of the most ornate Georgian houses in Norwich and of the two adjoining but structurally integrated dwellings have been restored, the cost being offset through the realization of the development potential of the land at the rear. The scheme was carried out by a private holding company for whom Rothermel, Cooke and Edwards were architects.[61] Further along Magdalen Street is the flyover that has caused so much indignation: the Norwich Society is co-operating in a scheme to make some temporary improvements to last until the space below the road can be filled with shops.

The wide range of the Architectural Heritage Year proposals indicates the extent of progress since the original Magdalen Street face lift scheme of 1959. Now, immediately adjoining the site of that experiment there is imaginative, yet sensitive, new development, conversion and restoration concentrated in an area large enough to contain a range of building types and ages but small enough for the effects of the effort to be readily evident. This time the project concerns the use and structure of the built environment, not just the cosmetic super-ficialities: comparison indicates the progress over sixteen years, yet this stage would not have been reached without the work of the pioneers of Magdalen Street on whose enthusiasm much has been built.

Conservation and the Future Development of Norwich

Half a century ago, it was suggested that 'in fifty years time Norwich will either not be worth looking at, or will be one of the most beautiful cities in England'.[62] At one time it looked as if the worst fears would be realized, as traffic and population pressures increased and out-of-scale road building and commercial developments threatened the city centre. Now, thanks to the vigilance of an increasingly large group of the environmentally aware, to the work of a distinguished group of architects and a dedicated City Planning Department, Norwich is increasingly achieving the recognition that it deserves. But recognition of this kind has constantly to be earned, for perfection demands constant vigilance.[63]

There have been many changes affecting the urban character. For a city of its size Norwich has a great number of shops, particularly quality shops, and banks, for it is capital of a large region. Over the years, the trade of its markets has increased but less local produce is offered for sale. Industrial growth and diversifi-cation has continued since the war, leading to the kind of soundly based economy that is essential if the urban fabric is to be properly maintained. Most of Norwich's industries are footloose and few are tied to the city by physical considerations; many of them are in the city because their founders were born or lived there. In these days of limited liability companies and large corporations there is little reason why they should stay unless they are encouraged to do so by good conditions.[64] The growth of the big companies and the age of the take-over has seen the removal to London and elsewhere of many head offices: many per-manent directors with roots in Norwich and a love for the city have been replaced by managers, transient, in East Anglia long enough to assist the region's economic growth but too briefly to put down roots in its old capital, present for far too short a time to become identified with or to learn to love the traditions of its environment.

Into that environment have come new buildings for new needs. Some are brashly unacceptable, yet have to be accepted; others, judged by their size and scale, silhouette and colour, texture and form, window and wall relationships, location and use are not merely acceptable, but welcome additions to the urban scene.[65] Norwich is beginning to realize its own qualities, to accept that advan-tages have to be paid for in terms other than those financial and to appreciate that the conservation and care of the old is only possible through the encourage-ment of all that is best in the new. 'Now, who can wonder that the children of that fine old city are proud of her, and offer up prayers for her prosperity?[66]

NOTES AND REFERENCES

1 Pevsner, N., *North-East Norfolk and Norwich*, Harmondsworth, Penguin, 1962, p. 204.

2 Ibid., p. 259–260.

3 Ibid., p. 205.

4 Ibid., p. 205.

5 James, C. H., Pierce, S. Rowland and Rowley, H. C., *City of Norwich Plan*, Norwich, 1945, p. 19.

6 Pevsner, op. cit., p. 205, gives the date as 1158, but the latest *Official Guide* (Norwich, 1973, p. 2) quotes 1194 for the award.

7 Pevsner, op. cit., p. 205.

8 *Official Guide*, op. cit., p. 3. This persists to the present day. It was commented on by H. V. Morton in *In Search of England* (London, 1927), and in the contemporary nickname of the local soccer club.

9 James, Pierce and Rowley, op. cit., p. 19.

10 *Official Guide*, op. cit., p. 6, and Leeds, Herbert, *Norwich, The City of Antiquities, Official Guide*, Norwich, 1924, p. 4.

11 East Anglia Regional Strategy Team, *Strategic Choice for East Anglia*, London, HMSO, 1974, figure 6.4.

12 Norfolk Joint Structure Plan Steering Committee, *Norfolk Joint Structure Plan: A Survey*, Norwich, 1974, Table 4.1, relates to employment exchange areas.

13 Morton, H. V., op. cit.

14 A survey in 1957 indicated that, in the holiday season, through traffic amounted to 24.5 per cent of that converging on the town centre: Buchanan, C. et al., *Traffic in Towns*, London, HMSO, 1963, para. 252, p. 114.

15 Morton, H. V., op. cit., p. 236.

16 Buchanan et al., op. cit.

17 In *The Listener*, 2nd January 1975.

18 Pevsner, op. cit., p. 232.

19 Betjeman, op. cit.

20 James, Pierce and Rowley, op. cit., p. 33.

21 By E. Boardman and Son, and Brierley and Rutherford, 1929–31. (See Pevsner, op. cit., p. 266).

22 1924, by Palmer, F. C. R. and Holden, W. F. C. (See Pevsner, op. cit., p. 272).

23 Goreham, G., *Yards and Courts of Old Norwich*, Norwich, n.d., page 3.

24 See McKie, R., 'Cellular Renewal: A Policy for the Older Housing Areas, *Town Planning Review*, Vol. 45, No. 3, (July 1974), p. 274 et. seq.

25 Green, Barbara and Young, Rachel, M. R., *Norwich—the Growth of a City*, Norwich, 1964, Map 7, facing p. 21.

26 Pevsner, op. cit., p. 274.

27 Cluer, A. and Shaw, M., *Former Norwich*, Attleborough, 1972, caption 5, page 10.

28 Ibid., p. 55 and p. 84.

29 Morton, H. V., op. cit., pp. 237–238.

30 *Fifty and Fighting: Norwich Society 1923–1973*, Norwich, 1973.

31 Pevsner, op. cit, p. 270.

32 Personal Communication from Mrs. Jean Ogden, Secretary, Norwich Society, 30.12.74.

33 Tillet, N. R., in the Foreword to James, Pierce and Rowley, op. cit.

34 James, Pierce and Rowley, op. cit., p. 12.

35 Ibid., p. 28.

36 Ibid., p. 55.

37 James, Pierce and Rowley, op. cit., pp. 126–130. The City Engineer acknowledged the importance of Magdalen Street and proposed a line that would involve the destruction of the architecturally less important west side. He noted that, if expense was no object, the more valuable buildings might be moved, or alternatively if the claim for retention of the buildings was greater than that for efficiency, a street parallel to Magdalen Street should be utilized as a by-pass as far north as his proposed inner ring road line.

38 Buchanan, C. et al., op. cit., pp. 112–123.
39 Ibid., p. 116.
40 Ibid., Figures 161 and 162 refer.
41 Wood, A. A., *Norwich Draft Urban Plan*, Norwich, 1967, p. 3.
42 Ibid., p. 5.
43 Ibid., p. 49.
44 Buchanan, et al., op. cit., Report of the Steering Group, para. 35.
45 James, Pierce and Rowley, op. cit., p. 1, map of Physical Characteristics of the Area.
46 This proposal was highly controversial and, were it to be revived today, it would no doubt succeed in uniting all those with aesthetic and civic interests in opposition: it is equally true that were it to have been built, it would after a century or so have become a respected landmark well loved by those same civic interests, rather as Pont Cysyllte is admired today.
47 Southern By-pass for Norwich, London, Department of the Environment, 1974.
48 Buro Goudappel en Coffeng b.v. and County Surveyor, Norfolk CC, *A Transportation Strategy for 1986, Issues and Possibilities*, Norwich, 1974.
49 Ibid., p. 5. p. 13.
50 Norfolk Joint Structure Plan Steering Committee, op. cit., and *Norfolk Joint Structure Plan: Issues and Possibilities*, Norwich, 1974.
51 Abercrombie, P. and L., *Stratford-upon-Avon, Report on Future Development*, Liverpool and London, 1923, p. 12.
52 Wood, op. cit., p. 38.
53 Wood, A. A., *Foot Streets in Four Cities. Report No. 3/November 1966*, Norwich, 1966.
54 Wood, A. A., *City of Norwich: Central Area Appraisal Report No. 1/May 1966*, Norwich, 1966, pp. 32–33.
55 Wood, A. A., *Norwich: London Street: the Creation of a Foot Street*, Norwich, 1969.
56 Pevsner, op. cit., p. 271.
57 Pevsner, op. cit., p. 249.
58 *Heritage over the Wensum*, a pamphlet produced by the City of Norwich briefly describes the project. Those involved include Colegate Investments Ltd., Magdalen Street and Anglia Square District Association, Norfolk Association of Architects, Norwich Corporation, Norwich-over-the-Water, Norwich Preservation Trust Ltd., and the Norwich Society.
59 Information kindly supplied by the architects.
60 Architects: the Norwich Partnership and Michael and Sheila Gooch.
61 The scheme was illustrated in *Building Design*, 20th December 1974, p. 4. See also Pevsner, op. cit., p. 273 for a description of the Magdalen Street frontage.
62 Morton, op. cit., pp. 237–8.
63 Sir Clough Williams-Ellis, in conversation with the author, Portmeirion, September, 1972.
64 James, Pierce and Rowley, op. cit., pp. 33–34.
65 See, for example, and the St. Michael-at-Pleas housing scheme, for which the architects were Edward Skipper and Associates.
66 George Borrow, quoted in Leeds and Herbert, op. cit., p. 3.

ACKNOWLEDGMENT

I would like to record my thanks for assistance received in various ways to Mr. Bernard Feilden and Mr. David Luckhurst of Feilden and Mawson, of Norwich; Mr. J. D. Grainger of the City Planning Department for information about 'Heritage over the Wensum', to Mrs. Jean Ogden, Secretary of Norwich Society, to Mr. and Mrs. G. A. Dunthorne of Long Stratton, to Mrs. N. Hannah of Hempnall, and to Miss Susan Dilley, formerly of the University of Nottingham. Like all visitors, professional and otherwise to almost any town in England I have been helped by Sir Nikolaus Pevsner's writing. Those who have helped or given information are in no way responsible for the views expressed, which are entirely the responsibility of the author.

Mr. Luckhurst kindly allowed me to reproduce his admirable drawing of the 'Heritage over the Wensum' site. The plan is based on one prepared in the City Planning Office and is reproduced with their permission. Photographs are by the author.

Conwy

History with a future

JOHN M. JONES

During the past five years or so much literature has been produced on conservation, its theory and purpose and the financial and administrative problems accompanying its implementation. Alongside this literature, and complementary to it, have been many practical demonstrations giving substance to these theories and resulting in the improved environments and care of buildings of architectural and historical interest. We have seen examples in many of our great historic cities such as York, Chester and Norwich. But these are well-known places which represent the large-scale architectural heritage which is dominated by cathedrals, churches, guild halls and the like. There has not been quite the same interest shown, measured perhaps by the amount of literature easily available to the public, in the smaller historic towns, a no less important part of our architectural heritage, but one of an essentially different kind, characterized not by architectural grandeur but by an intimate domestic scale. This type of 'lived in' architectural heritage is to be found in many of the smaller historic towns and settlements up and down the country and because people dwell and live out their lives within these towns they deserve just as much attention by the conservationists as the larger and more well-known places (Plate 21).

The historic walled town of Conwy on the North Wales coast in the County of Gwynedd is a very good example of this small-scale heritage. This article demonstrates, however, that, even in a small town, conflicts exist between the need for social and economic progress and the conservation of historic buildings and street patterns, and it serves to highlight the planning problems and the constraints and opportunities for conservation policy and practice that are met in planning for the future of this kind of town. But, while there are lessons to be learnt from a study of conservation in Conwy, as an example of small-scale heritage, Conwy is a unique township. And it is unique for several reasons. First, Conwy is an ancient monument of national importance. Secondly, Conwy is sited on a key river crossing point in North Wales and has a major traffic problem. Thirdly, while being a 'lived in' town it is also a major tourist attraction, and, fourthly, because of its geographical location and the presence of the city walls, access to the walled town is difficult and expansion beyond the walls is complicated. Because of these factors Conwy tends also to be unique in that it has perhaps received more publicity in relation to conservation than other towns of its size.

The Background to the Conservation Issues in Conwy

While publicity in local and regional newspapers has centred on the conservation issues just referred to, more importantly these issues have, during the past ten years or so, been the subject of several technical reports and studies. In 1967 the Collcon Study Group,[1] composed primarily of Welsh Office engineers, local government engineers and planners, carried out a detailed land use and transportation survey which considered various alternative routes for an expressway along the coast of North Wales and published its findings. Because Conwy is sited in a key position, it figures largely in the report of these findings. In 1969 the Civic Trust produced a report on tourism and conservation in Conwy.[2] In 1970, Conwy was the subject of a field study by students from the Department of Civic Design in the University of Liverpool and they too published a report.[3] In 1972 yet another report was produced, this time by R. Travers Morgan and Partners, which outlined their studies on the construction of a new improved route for the A55 trunk road and contained a statement by the Secretary of State for Wales regarding the 'preferred route'.[4] The most recent study is that of May, 1974 which is a report of the project team of senior officers of the Aberconwy Borough Council on the North Wales Expressway, as the new proposed A55 route has been referred to.[5] It is obvious from the nature of these reports and the discussions that have followed their publication that the problems peculiar to Conwy arise from both internal and external factors.

THE CIVIC TRUST REPORT OF 1969

Reasons for conservation often appear somewhat superficial. Those most popularly quoted in conservation reports are the traditional duty to protect and hand on a heritage to future generations in the belief that the past has something of value to offer, and the economic worth which historic buildings bring because they attract tourism to an area. Both of these reasons are important, the latter especially so in Conwy's case but, in Conwy, there are additional valid reasons for undertaking conservation.

In February 1968 the County Planning Officer for the County of Caernarvon (now part of the new County of Gwynedd), invited the Civic Trust to assist in the preparation of plans for the development of the town of Conwy with particular reference to the area lying within the ancient town walls. With agreement from the Wales Tourist Board the Trust recommended that a visitor interview survey should be carried out. The findings from this survey were combined with statistical information gathered from other sources and the Report, *Tourism and Conservation in Conwy* was produced. It had two aims, first to provide the planner with more information on tourist behaviour and the trends in tourism in Conwy and, secondly, to provide an example of the way in which a significant economic activity could be assessed alongside the need to conserve the historic fabric of the town. The Trust hoped that the suggestions and ideas put forward would interest those responsible for implementing the amenity improvement provisions of the Housing Act 1969[6] and the Development of Tourism Act 1969, both at that time very recent and timely statutes. The

Civic Trust Report stressed the paramount importance to the tourist industry of the physical appearance of Conwy. It was said that local residents were unable to afford to keep their houses in good repair and that day trippers, short stay visitors and holiday makers contributed very little to the town's economy. The solution was seen as promoting yachting, thereby, supposedly, introducing a large number of rich weekend yachtsmen into the town cottages, which would be converted and maintained in good repair. The social and economic implications of such a policy for the local residents of the walled town did not appear to have been taken into account. There was a distinct feeling in Conwy at that time that the report had been produced remotely from a London desk and that it had not really understood local needs and problems or really provided solutions to them.[7]

THE UNIVERSITY STUDY OF 1970

The Liverpool University study, which arose from a request by the Civic Trust, was an attempt to fill this gap in the Civic Trust Study, to give a more complete appraisal of the situation, and to make positive planning recommendations for consideration by Conwy Borough Council. A detailed physical survey of the land use, building fabric and visual condition of the walled town was carried out and recorded. Alongside the physical survey a sample social survey of the town's residents was conducted which concentrated on age structure, kinship and individual attitudes to the town. Evaluation of this survey information made it possible to construct a policy for the future of Conwy within the town walls, which paid attention not only to the physical fabric of dwellings, major town buildings, historic monuments and the overall environment, but also to traffic management and the social, particularly housing, and economic needs of the town's population. The physical and social surveys showed Conwy to have various problems which combined to reduce the benefits of living, working and taking recreation within the town. Problems were highlighted, such as the very small size of many houses, the lack of adequate amenities (and the cost of installing them), the annoyance and vibration from traffic on the main A55 trunk road which still passes right through the town, the growing number of cottages converted for holiday and weekend use by non-local people, the heavy dependence of shops on the holiday season and the serious number of eyesores in the form of derelict sites and pockets of neglected land in the area.[8]

The study stated broad principles of comprehensive area improvement and offered a way to the resolution of many of the areas of conflict which operate in Conwy; the conflict between second homes and local families, the conflict between through traffic and local traffic; the conflict between economic and physical progress. Above all, the need for planned change was stressed, together with conservation of an historic national asset and the unique atmosphere of the town.

It was acknowledged that the recommendations could not, in themselves, hope to solve all of Conwy's problems. Rather, they were presented for advice and encouragement, intended as a catalyst, to provide, at that time, a much needed platform for wider discussion among the various parties and organizations involved in the future of Conwy, the local Civic Society, the Borough Council and Conwy's residents. Back in 1970 the merits of the study, apart from its academic value, could not really be assessed.

The true measure of its success was to be judged some time later alongside the official reports, in terms of the debate and co-operation between the interested parties generated, and by the public involvement and participation in discussing the ideas put forward. It was hoped that, by promoting this wider discussion in Conwy, the broad principles of a comprehensive area improvement policy would be adopted. Striking the correct balance for the future between the three inseparable elements of community, history and recreation would ensure the survival of the flourishing local community within the context of the historic character of the borough and the tourism which has become so vital a factor in the economic life of the town.

THE TRAFFIC STUDIES: 1967–1974

The choice of a route for a new highway to replace the extremely congested A55, the main North Wales Coastal road, is of major importance in any discussion of conservation problems in Conwy. And it is really not surprising that 'after almost a decade of study, discussion and debate, opinion . . . remains deeply divided'.[9] There have been, as we have seen, a number of important reports setting out the pros and cons of different routes across the River Conwy. The routes most discussed in recent years are the 'Preferred Route' which would pass just south of the tubular railway bridge in Conwy and, still elevated, would skirt the south walls of the castle, passing along the Gyffin Valley into a tunnel which would emerge near the White Hart Hotel (Fig. 1). The motorway would in this instance run in very close proximity to the Castle walls and would greatly affect the view of the Castle. It would still, however, lie outside the walled town. The other major suggestion, put forward in the Collcon study, is to bridge the river away from Conwy at the mouth of the estuary. This would avoid intrusion into the environment of the Castle and south walls, but would greatly reduce the open aspect of the Conwy Morfa and the estuary.

Clearly a route which disturbs the fabric of Conwy itself would seem unacceptable and would make the task of conservation more difficult. Moreover, although the Castle is of a fairly large scale it is still wholly a part of Conwy itself and, in any case, the scale of a four-laned expressway running alongside the walls is out of keeping with the scale of the walls.

Nevertheless, in the University report, it was thought that if the through traffic from the A55 was removed, pressure on the walled town would be released, paving the way for effective conservation. However, since it is now unlikely that the re-routeing of A55 will occur before 1980 this should not affect the long-term prospects for conservation.[10]

Historical Heritage and Present Day Fabric

The foregoing short discussion of the basic issues affecting a conservation policy for Conwy, skim much too lightly over the fundamental factors concerning the town itself. Small-scale 'lived in' heritage demands a much closer examination, and Conwy is no exception if the best of the past is to be preserved within a modern setting.

The Borough of Conwy was founded in 1283 as part of Edward I's 'new towns' building programme in an attempt to settle the 'Welsh problem' and subjugate the Principality of North Wales.[11] It is a *Bastide* town, one of several around the coast of North Wales founded within a few years of each other, following upon the Statute of Rhuddlan, the others being Flint, Rhuddlan, Caernarvon, Harlech, Aberystwyth and Beaumauris. All belong to a category of urban foundations which were peculiarly characteristic of the thirteenth century. The years 1230–1350 were notable for the number of *bastides* and *villes neuves* set up by the sovereigns of France and their chief feudatories, in particular the English who were also the Dukes of Gascony. In fact, Edward I himself set up *bastides* to defend the marches of Guyenne,[12] so it is no accident, therefore, that Conwy should have many features in common with the *bastides* of France, especially since the works were supervized by James St. George, who had served with Edward I's cousin, Philip of Savoy, and who was probably the greatest military architect at that time.[13]

The new town of Conwy was located at the mouth of the River Conwy in order to hold a strategic position in controlling the major routes into Snowdonia along the Conwy valley and along the coast to Anglesey. The wisdom of this choice of location is emphasized by the fact that the present day major road and rail routes still pass through the town.

Its imposing castle and walls have remained substantially intact to the present day and it is one of the best preserved 'fortress towns' in Europe. The foremost historic building in Conwy is undoubtedly its castle.[14] It is one of the neat revenges of time that this monument, which for many centuries stood as a symbol of foreign domination and oppression, is now turned to the town's advantage, and acts as a lure for the descendants of the oppressors in search of recreation and of somewhere to spend their money. As it stands now, decorously fringed with neatly trimmed Department of the Environment lawns, the Castle has lost any reference to 'the concealed wounds of history'.

Conwy contains in addition, a number of buildings of architectural and historic interest (Fig. 1). Chief of these are: Plas Mawr, a fine Elizabethan mansion, Aberconwy House, a black and white timbered house of the same period, St. Mary's Church, originally the Church of a Cistercian Abbey confiscated at the time of the Borough's foundation; and Telford's suspension bridge built in 1826, a striking monument to the early Industrial Revolution and now in the care of the National Trust.

THE PLAN OF THE OLD TOWN

The Borough was planned as a complete unity and its present day streets preserve, almost intact, the plan as laid out in 1283. Apart from some minor infilling in the street blocks, very little change took place between the medieval period and the first quarter of the 19th century when there were two major alterations to the town's structure. Previously, the only landward entry into the town was

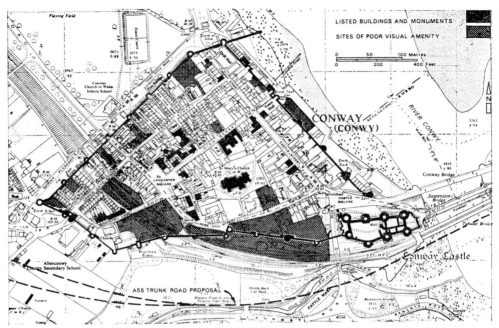

Fig. 1 Plan of Conwy, showing the location of the A55 trunk road proposal, sites of poor visual amenity and listed buildings (Crown copyright reserved)

via the Upper Gate and this remained until 1826 when Telford's road pierced the north west wall to enter what is now Lancaster Square. The second change came when, in 1848, the railway, which crossed the river in Robert Stephenson's tubular bridge, penetrated the south west sector of the town in a deep cutting necessitating the removal of some houses along Upper Gate Street and Rosemary Lane. The south wall was pierced by an arch and a tunnel was driven under the north west wall.

In the present century there have been some changes within the walled town, but most building in the Borough has taken place outside the walls in Gyffin, Cadnant Park and across the River in Deganwy. The opening of the new road bridge in 1958 had little direct physical impact on the walled town but has aggravated further the problems of traffic congestion in the town which have now become impossible at the height of the tourist season.

THE ARCHITECTURAL STYLE OF THE WALLED TOWN

The walled town has an interesting architectural vernacular style. Throughout, the commonest building material is a cement slurry and chipped stone rendering on stone or brickwork. Windows and doorways are picked out in smooth cement detailing and facades are usually washed or painted, often with the detailing in a contrasting colour. The majority of buildings are treated in this way. This vernacular 'Welsh Stucco' construction predominates in the area of terraced cottages in the north west of the walled town and among the larger buildings along the principal streets as in Lancaster Square and Castle Street. Stone and brick are far less commonly used, and the stonework is often whitewashed and there are a few other buildings constructed of materials ranging from timber to combination of tiles, brick and stone. Welsh slate is naturally the main roofing material but a few buildings are tiled.

The stucco cottages of the northwest area of the town are very similar to those in other small, old towns. On the main streets the number of reconstructions and additions over the years prevent any one style standing out. There are, however, a number of buildings which are very badly out of character. Notable are the telephone exchange, the Guild Hall, the Roman Catholic Church, the County Council Office, the Banks in Lancaster Square and a pair of semi-detached houses in Upper Gate Street, and a classroom at Aberconwy School, though this is a temporary construction. It is the unique scale and detailing of its cottage housing which gives Conwy a sense of visual unity and it is unfortunate, therefore, that poor examples have been allowed to intrude and create a confused visual effect. Plate 23 shows a row of houses unspoilt in this way.

HOUSING WITHIN THE WALLS

The condition of buildings is generally good and is being improved. The majority of houses now have standard basic amenities of hot and cold water, inside w.c. and bath and there has been much house improvement activity with government grant aid since 1967. In 1970 an attitude survey showed even then a wide knowledge of the improvement grant procedure and an enterprizing approach to it. Apart from improvements by local householders and landlords there were speculative conversions taking place at that time for holiday, weekend and retirement cottages for people from outside Conwy.

A change in 1974 to the policy on discretionary grants by the Borough Council meant that these were no longer to be awarded for second home improvements, conversion into holiday flats, and where an application is now made for a grant to convert a single dwelling into flats, evidence must be given to satisfy the Council that it is intended that these flats will be let as unfurnished accommodation to meet local housing needs.[15]

Building layouts are less satisfactory than the condition of the buildings. The very small size of the terraced cottages, usually with two rooms on each floor, provides only very limited accommodation. This has led to a number of 'two-into-one' conversions in a search for more space and a better layout. The small size, too, has contributed to the relative predominance of elderly persons and the lack of family units with children. However, the steep narrow staircases, the frequency of rising damp and the poor lighting in back yards are particular hazards for the elderly and these problems can only be partly solved by modernization. Externally the situation is little better. The tight layout of the back yards indicates the nature of the space standards' problem caused by the smallness of both the cottages and the building blocks. Often the steep topography as in the northwest aggravates the problem and means that houses are often cut into the ground and have only a narrow passage and retaining wall behind, thereby reducing both the light and the space for extensions to the dwelling. Some houses are built against the town walls which compounds the space problem. (Plate 22).

THE PROBLEM OF REAR ACCESS TO BUILDINGS

In the centre of the town the churchyard of St. Mary tends to seal off rear access to commercial properties in the High Street and Castle Street, although side access is reasonable and could be further improved with the clearance of out-buildings, as has been done with the Castle Hotel Yard. To the east of Castle Street, the town walls prevent rear access completely.

The restricted building layouts in the centre of Conwy, therefore, make it difficult to resolve the problem of access and reduce the scope for improvements and conversion. The best feature of the present layout is that it truly reflects the historic origin of the settlement as a medieval garrison, and, if it is considered that the small scale and close knit layout of the buildings are an integral part of Conwy as a national monument, then much careful thought should be given to any radical changes to the physical fabric. Because, however, of modern building standards requiring special provisions for fire regulations, it would not be possible to rebuild in a sympathetic scale or style at present densities and considerable thought will need to be given to the form and design of any new buildings.

Life in Conwy Today

In 1970, when the Liverpool University study was carried out, the population in the Borough of Conwy was about 12 000 persons of which 75 per cent lived in Deganwy and Llandudno Junction and less than a quarter lived in the walled town of Conwy itself. The town's present economy depends on three main sources of employment; fishing, tourism and holiday trades, and light industry at Llandudno junction. Social life in Conwy is dependent on age structure and on the attraction of Conwy for retired people and as a second homes' area.

CONWY'S ECONOMY

Fishing: Conwy's fishing fleet is small, consisting of five boats employing about 40–50 men, some only part time. The availability of mooring space on the quay is a limiting factor. 85 per cent of the Conwy's catch is taken directly to Billingsgate market in London. The remainder is sold locally and more profitably, especially in the holiday season. Fishing will never be a very large employer of labour in the area, because of the physical difficulties of enlarging the harbour facilities and increasing the number of boats. However, it will remain as a characteristic local occupation and the fishing fleet does have an incidental value in its attraction for visitors who enjoy looking at the boats and watching the catch being unloaded and packed. Plate 24 shows the harbour.

Tourism: Sited on the coast, near the Snowdonia National Park, Llandudno and other coastal holiday resorts like Colwyn Bay and Abergele, Conwy is a natural centre for tourist activities. Although it is not developed like these other places, tourism is a major support of the town's economy. This is particularly important for its shops and restaurants which receive a boost from tourist revenue in the summer, enabling an exceptionally high level of all year round shopping pro-vision for a town of Conwy's size (Fig. 2). The bulk of Conwy's visitors are

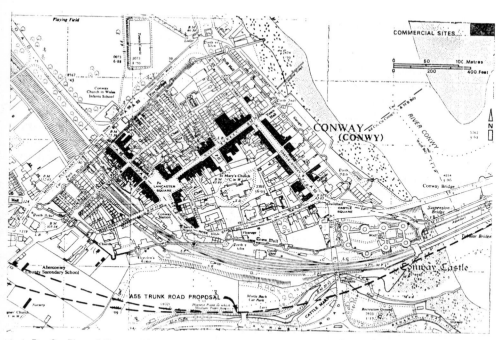

Fig. 2   Plan of Conwy, showing the location of commercial sites (Crown copyright reserved)

those who come for the day, attracted by its historic buildings, particularly the castle and town walls. Some come by coach, as Conwy figures regularly on holiday itineraries from the Gwynedd and Clwyd seaside resorts and beyond as far as Merseyside, but the majority come by car. The number of day trippers is likely to increase as communications between this area and Merseyside are improved by the new A55 proposals. For visitors who wish to stay longer, Conwy can accommodate some 7 400 holidaymakers, most of them in caravans, on a site away from the walled town on the Conwy Morfa, which is owned by the Borough Council and from which the Council derives a substantial annual income.

Conwy also attracts visitors as a sailing centre. The demand for berths at Conwy is heavy, and some of the town's cottages belong to yachtsmen. Conwy could quite easily become a major sailing centre for North West England and Wales and there have been several schemes for building marinas in association with other estuarine developments but it is not at all certain that the sailing boom of recent years will continue, and there are other considerations which throw some doubt on the future of the marina proposals. A marina would inject a lot of money into Conwy's economy but at what cost to the town's character? Few people, certainly not the local population, would wish Conwy to become exclusively a yachting town.[16]

Local Employment: Because it depends for part of its income on tourism, Conwy, like any other community in this situation, suffers from the problems of seasonal employment, which is lower in winter than in summer. The development of enterprises, such as traditional country crafts, which are seen to be increasingly popular with visitors, which do not require a high capital investment to initiate and which could be made to operate viably for only half the year during the summer months, would do much to remedy this problem. Conwy already has a number of shops selling traditional Welsh craft products and it is felt that this facet of the tourist trade could be further developed.

The only substantial source of male employment near Conwy is in the factories at Llandudno Junction. Other important employers in the area are the aluminium works at Dolgarrog, the County and Borough Councils, British Rail and the National Bus Company.

Conwy's economic future depends on its continuing popularity with tourists and on its power to attract more industry possibly into the Llandudno Junction area where there is already an industrial infra-structure developing. In spite of the higher costs of motoring and holidays, tourism is booming everywhere and there can be little doubt that a town of Conwy's charm and historical interest will continue to attract increasing numbers of day trippers and holidaymakers, particularly from the North West region.

SOCIAL LIFE IN CONWY

To try to understand the social basis of life in Conwy, the 1970 study involved the carrying out of a social survey. Its main purpose was to discover the attitudes of residents of the walled town to its character, fabric and social relationships. Questions put to the inhabitants took place on two distinct levels, that of the door to door survey questionnaire and that of formal interviews with some of the town's leading citizens. The nature of the information sought was as follows: age of respondent, length of residence in present house, previous place of residence, occupation of head of household, place of residence of relatives and children, car ownership and garaging, shopping habits and means of travel used, house tenure, rent and rates, amount of interest in improving dwellings, general attitudes to Conwy and attitudes to visitors.

The general picture which emerged was of a relatively, though not exclusively, elderly population. Within the walled town in particular many residents were of local origin, had lived in their present house for many years, and had numerous relatives living in the area. But this simple population pattern is changing as, attracted by its pleasant environment, an increasing number of professional and retired people move to Conwy from other areas. The attitude survey indicated that people like Conwy particularly for its character and location. Other important sources of affection for Conwy were long acquaintances with the town and the ties of family and friendship.

In spite, however, of this great affection for Conwy, the town was seen to have some drawbacks. Poor social facilities, traffic problems and other difficulties springing mainly from the growth of tourism were listed alongside the second homes' problem. Anxiety and resentment have been expressed at the rate at which cottages fall vacant, are bought up and converted to holiday cottages. There is good reason for this anxiety. While permanent settlers from outside can be an asset to the town, people who only use their Conwy house for a limited time in the summer are a liability. Cottages empty for most of the year provide little support for Conwy's traders; they give the town an unlived-in appearance and those living next door to an empty cottage suffer from coldness and dampness.

CONFLICTS OF INTEREST IN CONWY[17]

There are real conflicts of interest and opinion in Conwy on some matters. Many people want tourism to develop further while others would be inclined to restrict it. Some residents can suggest a number of changes they would like to see in the town while others are anxious that it should remain as it is. While these conflicts are undoubtedly real ones which would be difficult to overcome, it is possible that Conwy could work out a conservation policy which would satisfy most people. This would be one of controlled change, which would seek to preserve Conwy's good points while removing some, if not all, of its disadvantages.

Conservation Policy for Conwy

Until recently, conservation in Britain was mainly concerned with buildings and their preservation as part of the 'national heritage'. Such an approach is really only a new version of the preservation of public buildings by the use of special orders and statutory lists. Conwy is already well protected in this respect. The whole of the walled town was declared a conservation area in 1968. The Castle and Town Walls, Plas Mawr and Aberconwy House are Ancient Monuments. Also, a score or more buildings (including quite ordinary cottages) are listed as being of 'special architectural or historic merit'. Despite this enviable amount of protection, Conwy is facing the problems of a deteriorating physical fabric and the increase of visual eyesores (Fig. 1). The local environment is being seriously threatened by a growing traffic problem. And these are not the only problems. In common with many other historic towns, not enough attention is being given in Conwy to the social and economic needs of its residents.

In Conwy a different approach is needed to safeguard the environment of the walled town and the quality of life of its residents. Conwy is a community, not just a collection of separate buildings, and if, to outsiders, it is an attractive example of a complete and unique walled town, or a convenient yachting centre, to local people it is an intricate network of family and social relationships. This sense of unity is most important to any debate about an appropriate 'conservation policy'.

The 1974 Housing Act,[18] consolidating the Housing Acts since 1964, offers an answer to the environmental problems in Conwy with its provision for the creation of General Improvement Areas. This act gives power to local authorities to obtain not only the improvement of all substandard houses, but also of the physical and social environments, in any area designated by them as a General Improvement Area (GIA). The aim is to assist the residents to improve their own houses and, together, the whole area. With attention to the area as a whole, a greater number of house improvements could be expected than under a system

G

of individual enterprise and there would be the opportunity to carry out environmental works around the houses. Whole streets could be treated together saving time, money on administration and the actual contract work. A project such as this would not be entirely new expenditure because it must be remembered that a council already has power to make discretionary grants for house improvements. Within the framework of the GIA the following proposals directed mainly to the physical environment would be appropriate for the needs of Conwy at the present time.

A PHYSICAL PLAN FOR CONWY

Any conservation policy for Conwy must envisage the eventual removal of through traffic from within the town. We have already discussed the various schemes which do this, particularly the 'preferred route', which will run very close to the Castle walls raising important aesthetic considerations. Whichever route across the River Conwy is finally chosen, however, will mean that, before too long, through traffic, with all its environmental consequences, will be diverted from within the walled town, leaving the way open for a re-organization of circulation and the development of a pedestrian system (Fig. 3). In addition, the blighting effect of an earlier by-pass proposal (which was to replace the A55) and was routed along the quayside will be ended to allow improvement of this important economic and tourist asset.

Pedestrian Systems: If a pedestrian system is developed in Conwy, Lancaster Square together with the High Street, which contains Conwy's principal shops,

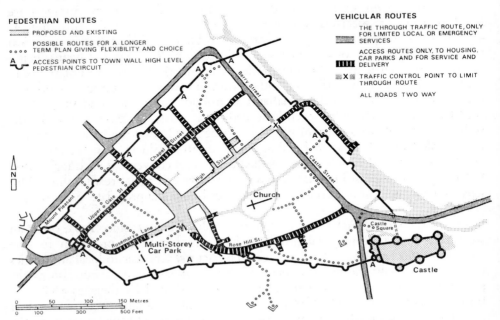

PEDESTRIAN ROUTES

▨▨▨ PROPOSED AND EXISTING

∘∘∘∘ POSSIBLE ROUTES FOR A LONGER
TERM PLAN GIVING FLEXIBILITY AND CHOICE

A ACCESS POINTS TO TOWN WALL HIGH LEVEL
PEDESTRIAN CIRCUIT

VEHICULAR ROUTES

▨▨▨ THE THROUGH TRAFFIC ROUTE, ONLY
FOR LIMITED LOCAL OR EMERGENCY
SERVICES

▥▥▥ ACCESS ROUTES ONLY, TO HOUSING,
CAR PARKS AND FOR SERVICE AND
DELIVERY

▨X▨ TRAFFIC CONTROL POINT TO LIMIT
THROUGH ROUTE

ALL ROADS TWO WAY

Fig. 3   Diagrammatic plan of Conwy, showing proposed and
existing pedestrian and vehicular traffic routes

could provide an admirable pedestrian precinct linking the commerce of the town with the quay which is a focal point for both local people and visitors. Much could also be made of existing footpaths in the town, extending them whenever possible. For example those through St. Mary's churchyard, now a pedestrian focus could be reinforced by linkages to High Street, Castle Street and Rose Hill Street.

Car Parking: Car parking cannot be provided within the walled town at the standards being adopted elsewhere (that is 1½–2 spaces per household by 1980). Local people must accept a compromise, which may be inconvenient but which should have real, if indirect, benefits on the town's atmosphere and environment.[19] At present, car parks are provided outside the town on the Morfa Bach site, and inside the walls at Castle Square, the Old Vicarage and the quayside. These are inadequate in the tourist season and it has been suggested by the Conwy Civic Society that additional car parks should be provided on the west side of Bangor Road on the old railway station site and on the cleared site of the 1937 memorial and chapel in Chapel Street, this would offer much needed relief for the immediate future but long term proposals might look to the development of a multi-storey car park on the site of the old station (Fig. 3). Because of the lower level of the site, this would afford the best opportunity to allow maximum car penetration within the walls with a minimum of tarmac desert.

The proposed pedestrian system will inevitably reduce the number of car parking spaces within the walled town and will increase the pressure on the Morfa Bach car park. The Borough Council plans to build a footbridge over the railway to give access to Morfa Bach through the Porth y Felin gate (at present giving access to a scrapyard, which is to be removed). The continued use of Morfa Bach would, of course, depend on the choice of one of the alternative Expressway routes planned to cross the estuary at Deganwy, and not the 'preferred route'.

Service and Rear Access: Service access must allow penetration to a maximum of 30 metres from all dwellings (for refuse collection, etc.) and must permit occasional movements by fire-engines, ambulances and other such emergency vehicles. The use of carefully sited, removable, bollards should give adequate access to dwellings without allowing cross-town traffic to penetrate the residential part of the walled town. A problem will arise, however, over the rear servicing of business premises in High Street and unless this is designed carefully it could conflict with the use of the churchyard as a pedestrian focus.

In most of Conwy, houses are right on the street and there is no space in which to make a satisfactory transition from the street to the living area of the dwelling. At the back of the houses, in contrast, service rooms open out on to a yard, an entry passage, or even a vacant area (Fig. 4). In a programme of house improvements, these back areas could be improved by, for example, re-decoration of rear facades, and the repair of neglected outbuildings. It might be possible in the residential part of the town to use funds for 'environmental works' for the creation of rear courtyards by the removal of unwanted sheds, party walls and the incorporation of the many small waste plots at present unused. Sun-traps in

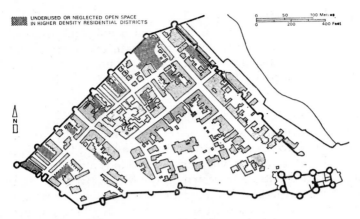

UNDERUSED OR NEGLECTED OPEN SPACE
IN HIGHER DENSITY RESIDENTIAL DISTRICTS

Fig. 4   Plan of Conwy, showing underused or neglected open
space in high density residential districts

these areas would be suitable for placing public seats for use by elderly people, while the open space created would provide safe children's play areas, a focus of contact between mothers.

Urban Landscape: More generally, it will be helpful to include provision for some landscaping to reduce the visual length of streets and to define points of activity and communal interest, such as Lancaster Square, High Street, the Churchyard and the Quay. Any new planting or redesigned street paving will need to be concentrated in sheltered, favoured points, as suggested for the more secluded spaces in the residential area. This is better visually and helps maintenance and, hopefully, the control of wilful damage. Care needs to be taken to phase all landscape and environmental works in with the house improvements programme and, of course, to design them in sympathy with the best elements of the existing fabric and town-scape.[20]

Conwy is remarkable for its almost complete girdle of walls which give a strong visual unity to the town, and serve as a tourist attraction. The Department of the Environment (DOE) plans to open up the walls to the public as a scenic walk.[21] When this work is complete, the walls will provide a fine vantage point from which to view the town and the estuary and this is an added reason for making better use of the pockets of derelict land which adjoin part of the wall but also the DOE could be approached concerning the placing of seats, the creation of easier access and possibly the use of lighting to improve the walls as an asset for all to use and enjoy.

PROTECTING CONWY'S SMALL-SCALE QUALITY

The finely moulded 'urban grain' of Conwy is one of its most precious, yet most vulnerable assets. The scale, the sense of enclosure and the visual unity of a street facade are all in delicate balance. While some intrusion by bad building form can be absorbed, a series of gaps and breaks cannot. This also applies to undue variety in decoration and detailing, notably of shop fronts. It is essential also for existing building lines to be maintained. Regimented uniformity is not needed but rather an intelligent and sympathetic use of development control and building regulations. By adopting from the outset a sensitive approach to planning control, the small-scale quality which is Conwy's heritage will be protected.

Conservation with a Human Face

The conservation policy outlined sets out to reconcile the growth of tourism and other pressures for change in a controlled way. It is a policy orientated to the needs of the people who live in Conwy and it will depend for its success on their active participation. If it does succeed they will be ensuring that those changes which occur are controlled in their own interests and, of course, the tourist will benefit as well, for a town made more pleasant and convenient to live in will also be a better and more attractive place to visit.

This chapter has, it is hoped, shown that the historic town of Conwy, but way been neglected. Technical reports have been prepared, studies have been made and opinions have been given, not only by the residents of Conwy, but by their elected representatives, by societies interested in the welfare of Conwy and by local newspapers. From these reports, studies and opinions it has become clear that action could be taken to implement a conservation policy outlined above. It is also clear that, if a conservation policy depends for its success on active participation by the Conwy people, then there is ample evidence to show that it should not be difficult to establish the right atmosphere to enable this to take place. What is evident, too, is that this active participation should ensure that Conwy will not become a museum piece but will continue to be a 'lived in' historic town with, it is to be hoped, a much improved domestic character.

NOTES AND REFERENCES

1 Welsh Office, *Collcon Traffic Study*, Cardiff, Welsh Office, 1968.
2 Civic Trust, *Tourism and Conservation in Conway*, London, Civic Trust, 1968.
3 Department of Civic Design, The University of Liverpool, *Conway: History with a Future*, Liverpool, 1970.
4 Morgan, R. Travers and Partners, *A55 Feasibility Study and Preferred Route Report*, London, R. Travers Morgan and Partners, 1972. The terms of reference of this report were 'to examine and report on the construction of a new of improved route for the A55 trunk road generally between St. Asaph and Aber, ... taking into account the findings of the Collcon Traffic Study and the representations made thereon by local authorities'.
5 Aberconwy Borough Council, *North Wales Expressway: Report of Project Team*, Llandudno, 1974.
6 *Housing Act 1969*, London, HMSO, Part II, s. 28.
7 Senior, Michael, 'Tourism and Conservation in Conway', *North Wales Weekly*, 18 June 1970.
8 Department of Civic Design, op. cit., pp. 21–23.
9 Aberconwy Borough Council, op. cit., Foreword to the Report.
10 Department of Civic Design, op. cit., p. 62. A Public Inquiry to consider the route of the proposed A55 Expressway is now sitting.

11 Carter, Harold, *The Towns of Wales*, Cardiff, University of Wales Press, 1965; Tucker, Norman, *Conway and its Story*, Denbigh, Gee and Son, 1960; Edwards, J. Goronwy, 'Edward I's Castle-Building in Wales, *Proceedings of the British Academy*, Vol. 32, 1946, pp. 15–81.

12 Evans, Joan, *Art in Mediaeval France*, London, 1948, p. 223.

13 Morris, A. E. J., 'Bastide Towns', *Official Architecture and Planning*, Vol. 30, No. 9, (September 1967), pp. 1311–1319.

14 Edwards, J. Goronwy, op. cit., p. 37; Ministry of Public Building and Works, *Conway Castle and Town Walls*, London, HMSO, 1968.

15 Aberconwy Borough Council, Minutes of Council Meeting, 25 May 1974.

16 Jessop, R., *Boating in North Wales*, Manchester University Thesis, unpublished; '£30m. Conway Riverside Developments Plan', *North Wales Weekly*, 1 May 1971; 'Council to Consider Rival Marina Schemes', *North Wales Weekly*, 8 May 1971; 'Model of Rival Marina', *North Wales Weekly*, 22 May 1971.

17 Senior, M., op. cit.

18 *Housing Act 1974*, London, HMSO. Parts IV, V, VI deal with district scale improvement powers. A distinction is drawn between areas suitable for broadly based environmental action under General Improvement Area (GIA) procedures and the new Housing Action Area (HAA) procedures. The local authority may assist associations and individuals to undertake 'Environmental Works' beyond the scope of house improvements, 50 per cent being paid by central government subject to a general limit of £50. Parts VII and VIII consolidate the improvement grant system as it affects the individual property owner. Second homes no longer qualify for grant aid. The major change from previous legislation is the attachment of conditions to grants so as to ensure that the improvements benefit owner-occupiers or tenants, not speculators.

19 'Points from Parking Restrictions Plan to be Reconsidered', *North Wales Weekly*, 23 September 1971.

20 'Civic Society Takes Close Look at Conway', *North Wales Weekly*, 3 December 1970.

21 Conwy Castle and its walls are under the control of the Department of the Environment, which is carrying out a programme of restoration including improving public access. It is the Department's policy gradually to improve the views to and from the walls.

The Derbyshire heritage

The conservation of ordinariness

JOHN NELSON TARN

This chapter is concerned with what might be called the conservation of ordinariness. It is written with the problems of Derbyshire and the Peak District National Park in mind, but the points which it raises might be made about a number of rural areas in England where the pressures for recreational facilities, for second homes or rural homes, for the resolution of regional transportation issues and the implication of natural resources could equally be paralleled. It also presents very clearly the great paradox that things which are not necessarily of great intrinsic architectural merit are themselves worthy of conservation because of their value in a broader setting, as part of the street, or as buildings in a landscape. As in most discussions of conservation issues I do not want to consider the idea of conservation simply as a matter of static preservation, but to look at it in the broader context of an on-going positive planning attitude and I am becoming increasingly conscious that, as a basic philosophical issue, it is no use discussing conservation unless at the same time one has a firm eye to the future well-being of the area under discussion, to the economic problems which exist or which may be generated by a conservation policy and to the well-being of the community as a whole, particularly the existing locally-based population.

The Nature of Rural Conservation

It is also no use talking about conservation anywhere, but particularly in country areas, unless one addresses the discussion to individual people. The principal conclusion which I hope I can draw is that, in a rural setting, conservation issues are issues of supreme physical delicacy. They require, therefore, the active concern and participation of ordinary people who own simple properties. So I will make a plea for education and a wide dissemination of information and knowledge to all those who are concerned with life in the countryside; simply because without their co-operation the sophisticated views of conservation which might be expressed by professional people and experts will be of no avail. There is, in fact, no adequate machinery for ensuring that the conservation of our villages will actually take place, except the machinery of goodwill and the growing interest and concern of the public at large. Perhaps this is much more relevant in rural than in urban areas, since the decisions of the individual in situations where beauty is certainly no more than skin deep are important and quite irrevocable. Perhaps, also, one is arguing for a higher standard of every-day design: in fact for a new vernacular style of building appropriate to the 1970s.

Rural conservation, then, raises a whole series of questions which are perhaps different in degree from those of the town, as well as a number which are also different by nature. Very often it is not possible to distinguish between the amalgam of natural beauty and man-made building heritage, because the two are inextricably inter-related. What part of our landscape, as we know it, is 'natural', for example and how far are we deceived by historical perspective? Built character traditionally grows out of the landscape both in what might be called organic terms—that is traditionally the way in which buildings sit in the landscape and are governed by its contours and characteristics—and through the fact that the locally available materials have become, with the passage of time, the accepted building materials of that area. Even the lack of obvious materials has often given rise to an alternative but recognizable character. The character of many a small coastal town in the south-west, Dartmouth for example, or Polperro on a smaller scale, is established by the escarpments and ravines which not only create the natural harbours and, therefore, give rise to the reason for the community, but are also seen as a challenge to man in his attempts to locate buildings and create communities. In the same way the development of flint walling techniques and decorative pargetting in East Anglia are good and obvious examples of building methods which result from the absence of more suitable materials, and ultimately a local style of considerable attractiveness results. This same problem encouraged the development of brick in Eastern England and that also led to a precocious understanding of its potential. Man is, therefore, quite capable of making virtue out of necessity and building history has proved this over and over again.

Quite the reverse is probably true in the Cotswolds, where technique and a style of building is entirely the result of a long dialogue with a readily available and very malleable local stone which gives an all-pervading visual harmony to a sweeping belt of countryside. This has encouraged a prodigious amount of well-designed building which in its turn reflects the affluence of much of that part of England. It may be a coincidence that the availability of a good building stone in this case is linked with a rich agricultural area, but the outcome for whatever reason is a building tradition which is distinctly recognizable and which has its root firmly in the discipline which the material has inculcated as the masons worked with it over many centuries.

It is possible, then, to establish logical reasons why, historically, much of our countryside is the way it is. But just as in the town, this pattern of development which over many centuries has been modulated stylistically to give variety of visual textures as well as local character, so in the countryside the modern way of building and the new physical patterns of development are subject to strong regional and even national pressures, to changing social circumstance and to transport revolutions, to altering life styles and shifting economic problems. Furthermore, the concept, as well as the reason, for local character and vernacular styles has now, to all intents and purposes, vanished: it is often cheaper to buy bricks made 300 kilometres away than to quarry stone from a nearby hillside and it is difficult to persuade many people that a rural community is not physically or socially a suburb. It is also difficult to persuade road engineers that random verges and non-standard details are often essential if any sense of personality is to survive. The traditional vitality of character in rural England is rooted firmly in the peculiarities and idiosyncracies of each district and in a variety of building methods which have long since become accepted practice. Today many of these methods are dying out and it is difficult in some areas to find craftsmen who understand the traditional techniques of building. In Derbyshire it is now surprisingly hard to find masons who understand how to point up traditional gritstone walls or who know how to build dry limestone walls and there are more examples of malpractices in techniques of building in the countryside than many urban people would credit.

The Character of the Derbyshire Landscape

Derbyshire, particularly that part of it which has been designated since 1949 as a National Park, might be an area of natural beauty whose quality is universally recognized as quite outstanding, but it is not free from the pressures which beset most other rural areas and particularly those which lie on the fringes of major conurbations. The Park is seen as a rural lung and it has peculiar value because of its amalgam of great scenic qualities and attractive rural communities. But it is, nevertheless, an area in which people live and, indeed, have lived and earned their livings long before a National Park was created. Sometimes one suspects that this simple fact is nearly forgotten. It is an on-going community with many problems of rural economy which local people often feel are exacerbated by its National Park status and which are sometimes overlooked in the arguments about the conservation of natural beauty which are laid upon a Planning Board. Furthermore, when one examines the building fabric and the make-up of the villages which lie within the Park, many of them are no more memorable than those of many country districts. Here, perhaps, is the start of this concept of ordinariness, but it is fortunate in some ways that they *are* seen as special, because this permits a low key rural fabric to be quietly husbanded. But we should be clear that many of the problems faced in Derbyshire are those of rural England generally rather than of some peculiar special architectural heritage. It is also true that groups of buildings or whole villages of purely vernacular interest are more at risk from eroded change than are listed buildings and architecturally more famous places.

Agriculturally, the uplands of Derbyshire have never been particularly prosperous—indeed for much of its history this has been a poor area where even valley farming is a hard-won thing and so it has not generated a great heritage of elaborate buildings. Much of the Park, in fact, can be distinguished as upland country although not all of it is moorland and, because of this, there is for many people a harshness of character which is generated by a fairly tough climate and at first sight a dour landscape. It is only in the southern valleys and towards the Trent plain that the Derbyshire scene is soft and gentle. Many people see it as by no means the most friendly of countrysides. It is inappropriate to approach conservation here as an issue which is concerned with a soft mellow attitude towards building technique. The Derbyshire village is a north country village and it has a straightforward character which is as much the product of climatic considerations as of building materials.

H

BUILDINGS AND TEXTURE

It is important and significant that the second half of the seventeenth century was the period when Derbyshire achieved economic stability. The gentry and the yeoman farmers started a concerted building programme which began to produce a recognizable architectural character which is characteristically old-fashioned and out of date and at the same time stamped with a recognizable local vernacular character. The most famous houses, like Chatsworth, are rebuilt in the 'court-style', but this does not filter through to smaller buildings until much later. The vernacular is an architectural language of a particular social class, and in more sophisticated places it would be categorized as distinctly rustic. Its no-nonsense approach to ornament and decoration is socially appropriate and environmentally practical. One is as necessary as the other.

But the visitor schooled in the wool districts of East Anglia, Somerset and the Cotswolds who expects a multiplicity of grand country houses and dominant late Gothic churches will, on the whole, be disappointed. Tideswell church is outstanding here, where it would be unexceptional elsewhere. Eyam Hall, a major manor house of the late seventeenth century, is one of a handful of stylistically complete and formal designs and the overgrown farmhouse version of a manor, like Youlegreave, is typical of many important houses which might pass without much note in other parts of England. Most of the Derbyshire communities are modest in scale as well as character. They are built of local stone which alternates dramatically between the warm gritstones and the cool white limestones. The visitor who traverses the Peak Park at different times of the year will soon come to recognize that these stones take on quite different seasonal characteristics. In summer the gritstone appears warm and mellow and the limestone has a cold appearance; but in winter the gritstone becomes almost sullen in character and the limestone achieves a variety of textures and colours which it does not seem to possess at other times in the year. It is also an important characteristic that as you pass from one valley to another you can also pass from one stone belt to another and so the character changes suddenly and dramatically. The soft, well-wooded landscape of the gritstone areas gives way to the bald landscape of the limestone belts, often quite lacking a significant vegetation, where you feel that the limestone is only barely covered with earth. The whole surface of the countryside seems to be littered with limestone regularly gathered together to make walls, sometimes lying loose in piles, sometimes raising itself up into recognizable buildings. There are few places in England where the influence of locally available building materials is so clearly implied in the dynamics of the natural character of the landscape and its buildings. The walls around the fields and the stone used for the farms and the villages themselves all bear witness to the locally available material and, at the junction between stone belts you find, predictably, an ambivalent use of stone building techniques. Here limestone and gritstone are used indiscriminately for mass walling although it is usually possible to discern that gritstone is used almost universally for angles and junctions, for quoins and jambs, lintols and cills and the limestone is used for infill. This is a practical proposition in building terms. So the relationship between the way the hillsides are divided up by hedges or walls and the way the villages are built are usually linked, which is a reminder that the character of the landscape is rooted in its underlying geology as much as is the form of the buildings. Here the tradition begins and here it also ends (Plates 25–28).

THE IMPACT OF INDUSTRY

But, just as Derbyshire has gained its character, as do so many parts of this country, from its own locally available materials, so now in the twentieth century these very materials generate problems which are of more than local interest. Mineral extraction is nothing new in Derbyshire and there are innumerable memorials of the lead mining industry in the last century. But now the quarrying of limestone particularly goes on on a grand scale. There are other mineral deposits, and the Planning Board sighted 150 mineral workings within the Park itself.[1] It is not simply a problem of mining which is visually relatively un-damaging but of open-cast working, of extracting large chunks of limestone hillside and scarring the already exposed landscape permanently. The lead mines are now overgrown and their buildings, crisp examples of good straightforward engineering design, were entirely built in local materials and are of considerable interest for the industrial archaeologist. Indeed, they are a subject for conservation in their own right. The quarries and cement works, by contrast, are not only causing considerable local environmental pollution now with dust, smoke and noise but they are leaving the countryside pockmarked and permanently scarred. Many believe that the interests of the National Park are ill-served by the extraction of minerals even though this provides badly needed employment. It will be a matter for continuing debate whether the national need for minerals transcends the local need for recreation and physical attractiveness. Time will also tell whether the right to extract minerals should also carry with it the burden of restoring the landscape at the end of the day. But who ultimately pays for this and when will the decision on ultimate values be taken? The earth provides the reason for character, it provides wealth and employment: it can also be exploited and just as industry once destroyed the joy of urbanism it may also debilitate the countryside itself.

Industrial intrusion also brings local problems of transport. As the railway network declined so has the importance of road communications increased. But heavy lorries do not travel easily down country lanes and it has become necessary to conserve the plant life of verges and hedges for they are as much at risk as are the buildings.

It is instructive, however, to contemplate the attitude most people take to the railway even in country areas. The Ashbourne to Buxton line is a good example. Constructed through difficult railway country, it was closed in recent years only to be seen now as an important and desirable link, too expensive to re-open. It did violent things in Monsaldale and it is still possible to see quite clearly how this superb valley was altered by cuttings and embankments to facilitate its passage. But now the earthworks have matured, in landscape terms, and they are tolerated, while the more brash viaduct is actually the subject of conserva-tionist pleas! This much does human nature shift in its attitude with the passage of time and a hint of romance.

Conflicting Issues in the Peak District National Park

Around the edge of this great area of natural beauty lie the predators, the conurbations of Manchester and South-East Lancashire, Sheffield and the Yorkshire
towns, Chesterfield, Derby and the Potteries—a great ring of urban settlements
all of which have expanded rapidly since the industrial revolution. For those
who live in these towns the Peak District can mean not only an area of natural
beauty to be admired and enjoyed in a contemplative sense, but also a place for
recreation and enjoyment in a more extravert and practical way. To those who
live and work in one of these great conurbations the Park can alternatively, be
seen, at worst, as an obstacle to easy communication with places on the opposite
side.

The reason for the Park begins as we have seen with its landscape character.
It is situated in the foothills of the Pennines and its roads are winding country
tracks or at best hazardous and statistically inadequate main traffic arteries which
are difficult to negotiate with large vehicles and, for the rapid motorist, the
scene of frequent holdups and hazards. The roads, traditionally, have negotiated
the complex terrain almost solely at the scale of the horse and cart. They cross
rivers by ancient narrow bridges and they pass logically through narrow village
streets, none of which were designed for current traffic volumes. Topographically,
they naturally take the easiest route, but there are often few alternatives in this
difficult terrain. To those anxious to reach the other side of the Park the network
of roads in the Peak is nothing short of a menace, but to those who wish to
linger in the countryside, to move from place to place slowly and by roads
which are in scale with the landscape, the traditional pattern has much to
recommend it.

While the journey across the Park can be aggravating, those who seek leisure
here will also find that as they penetrate from one side they meet fellow travellers
from the opposite side. The Park is never large enough to cope with those who
seek its isolated spots and year by year it receives increasing numbers of visitors,
often frustrated by each other. Ideally, and at best, it is a place of peace and quiet
where you can get away from it all, but if you go on the wrong days you find
that you meet far too many other people. Evidently everybody wants to drive
down the Goyt or to picnic in the Winnats—most people seem to wish to shop
in Bakewell on market day and there is nowhere left to park your car. All the
climbers in the Midlands wish to climb the few available Edges and there are
few crevices of solitude. We turn the whole Peak into some great honeypot, but
we shall find it distasteful when the grass is trodden off the banks of the Dove
by human feet. The traffic builds up to such quantities in some places that the
only reasonable solution is a recourse to traffic management schemes such as
those in the Goyt valley where personal liberty is restricted in order to provide a
traffic free environment for the majority. If the Park is to be a place with open
access to most people then there is a price to pay in terms of management, both
of people and of vehicles. But is it necessary to organize the countryside as
though it was a municipal park? It may be necessary to provide car parks and
discreet lavatories, but should everything be carefully signposted and the foot-

Fig. 1 General map of Derbyshire and the surrounding area, showing the proximity of major towns and conurbations

paths so well organized that they are without hazard and incident for those who are used to such things in the towns. Do these organized amenities constitute an infringement of the very nature of the countryside and does this not mean that we are in a very minor way destroying the character which we set out to admire, simply by artificial and precocious sophistication? This sort of erosion of natural quality is a part of the whole conservation problem and is clearly a sensitive area, where judgment and relative values are as important as in more overtly built situations.

On the other hand, if a whole region is laid open to the public this cannot imply that normal agriculture can cease. The uplands are important both for sheep farming and for forestry work, the valleys for normal farming, and the people who live and work in the Peak District need some assurance that they can continue their traditional occupations despite the arrival of frequent visitors. It is all too easy to consider the farmer, or the village schoolmaster and the postmistress as some kind of mobile rural museum rather like Marie Antoinette's perfumed sheep at Versailles and it is perhaps difficult to realize that they are fulfilling a real social function in developing communities which must go on when the visitors depart, either for the night or for the winter. The community is a social as well as a physical thing and it exists to generate and regenerate itself as well as to service visitors and perhaps gain a growing livelihood from erosion.

In addition to the visitor, there is the growing problem of the urbanites who actually live in the country and commute daily over the hills to labour in one or other of the great conurbations, returning at night to their rural suburbia or their romantic cottages all carefully muted in character by the constraints of the Planning Board. But negative building, fulfilling the basic colour sequences of the vernacular style in sham materials, does not constitute a realistic extension to village structure either physically or socially. The new houses, complete with their picture windows and standard wrought-iron gates, set up in tidy rows as detached boxes, in streets which fulfil every requirement of the traffic engineer and are lit at night by glaring sodium lights, are just as alien to the true character of the countryside as the vamped-up rural cottage and the badly converted barn with its jarring green shutters decorated with fretwork hearts, with phoney brass carriage lamps on either side of the fully-glazed frontdoor, itself complete with bull's eye glass in crudely astragalled panes. It is not necessary to carry the parody as far as the cart wheels set in the gates and the plastic gnomes in the garden —all of which exist in abundance—to realize that much of this is in fact suburban development set in the countryside. It is alien and unconvincing (Plate 30).

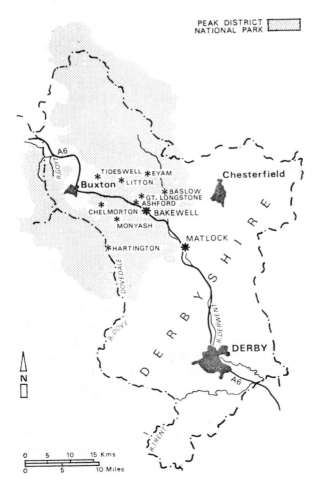

Fig. 2 Map of Derbyshire, showing the area of the Peak District National Park, the route of the A6 trunk road and the location of places mentioned in the text

A Sensitive Basis for Rural Conservation

The countryside and the village are not just simply under pressure, then, they are now under seige and, paradoxically, although Derbyshire is sufficiently beautiful to be recognizably outstanding, its built heritage is so modest as to be at the point of self-effacement and the fabric is so fragile and delicate as to be in constant peril. Rural building here is a masterpiece of understatement, which is precisely what makes it vulnerable. I have approached the problem of built conservation from an underlying natural geological basis because my main contention is, first, that rural conservation must always be seen as a dialogue between landscape and building, between what we inherit and what man has made of it from time to time. Secondly, in these rural areas it is not possible—indeed it would be foolish—to define character by the normal architectural analytical processes based upon style; we are thrown back upon a closer scrutiny of vernacular details and the relationship of buildings to one another as well as to the spaces that are created between them. In a town, one might talk of the tension generated in the street, but here we should recognize the problems associated with relaxing that tension to a point where it is sometimes hard to describe exactly what holds a space together.

Derbyshire does possess a variety of country characteristics from the bleak Pennine uplands stretching across to the flat valley of the Trent which is clearly 'southerner' in character. The Peak Park does not stretch quite that far but the contrast between the uplands and the valleys is sharp: Dovedale and the gentler stretches of the Derwent, as well as villages like Ashford and Baslow are clearly a different world from the windswept villages of the hills such as Monyash, Litton and Chelmorton. The villages that shelter under the Edges like Eyam and the communities in the central uplands like Tideswell and Hartington contribute to the wealth and variety of village concepts. The swift changes of character from the gritstone to limestone only intensify this sense of variety created by siting conditions. In the gritstone areas I have already pointed out how the earth itself feels thicker and softer over the rocks, the vegetation more fulsome, the buildings softer and darker. The limestone country seems, by contrast, like an emaciated carcass, the bones and sinews much more evident, the stone dominates the vegetation, and the field boundaries running on for mile upon mile in dry walling as though they dominate the earth itself linking farms and barns into a consistent landscape. It is almost as though the minor buildings are beads in some gigantic necklace made up of walls, while the villages are a kind of pendant or ornamental detail. It is here, perhaps, that it is best to pursue further the quest for building character. Limestone is a coarse stone by nature, used most frequently as a random dry walling material or roughly coarsed. Most frequently for all but the simplest of buildings it is used in conjunction with gritstone so that the detail can be carefully dressed or larger blocks can be used in place of the small rough pieces of limestone. The buildings are usually low with small spans and uniform pitched roofs, the openings typically wide rather than high. The feeling is of breadth and solidity, where the relationship of a generously proportioned window to wall gives the appearance of strong load-bearing structure. The gables frequently rise above the verge to protect it, corbel brackets and a flat cap to the gable are the only details. The gritstone buildings vary this pattern a little: the quality of the walling may reach careful ashlar and the more malleable sandstone will take a fine moulding on a mullion or transom and there may be a simple string course and hoodmould. In the typical building and, indeed, even in the more prestigious manor houses of the seventeenth century there is probably little more ornament and detail. Doorways are particularly restrained in character. At this level we are discussing the rural domestic style of Derbyshire, but the characteristics are those of many rural areas and, apart from particular proportional qualities and local corbel details, I cannot detect anything specifically 'Derbyshire'. Those who care about it are sensitive to these simple qualities just as they can recognize the harmony of grouping techniques where farm house and barn are repetitive structures in essence. It is possible to recognize a favourite proportion in some Derbyshire farmhouses where the horizontal emphasis both in the shape of the building and the proportions of the windows seems to be more characteristic than in other parts of the country, but this is a nuance and the real character is vested in the materials: in stone.

Because these qualities are so simple and reticent it is extremely easy, at a time when traditional craft skills are declining, to find well-intentioned repairs resulting in diabolical changes in appearance—harsh new pointing, standing proud of the stone and often done in neat cement—or the replacement of original multi-paned sliding sash windows with picture windows or 1930s style casements. Many of these changes are deemed to be improvements by the owners and most would be hurt to know that they are destroying the character of the building in which they live. Fashion has always been a great modifier of buildings throughout history, but it is unfortunate that fashion now has a national quality and that window details, particularly, have overtones and connotations which are, to say the least, unfortunate when they are seen indiscriminately in suburban towns and country villages. They do nothing to maintain let alone enhance the character of the street, nor do they help to retain the existing scale and appearance of the buildings. The replacement of multi-paned windows by single sheets of glass, or perhaps two large sheets, alters the scale of most eighteenth and nineteenth century cottages in a most dramatic way. The task of attempting to create a better sense of historical awareness and a feeling for fitting design amongst the public and to demonstrate how these minor alterations are destructive, is an essential part of the educational problem of conservation: it is, in fact, the only weapon that the planner possesses, as he is helpless through the normal machinery of planning to control minor alterations to windows in the average cottage. It is neither realistic nor sensible to create blanket conservation areas and the maintenance of the rural fabric becomes finally a matter of husbandry, good building practice and wise education to foster a new level of popular taste. Domestic architecture in a typical Derbyshire village is, in fact, the architecture of the builder rather than the architect and it is in a tradition which is never precocious. The character is elusive and delicate and the impact of the building is nothing except in relationship to its neighbours (Plates 25–28).

THE NEED FOR A NEW VERNACULAR

It seems right to stress first the ordinary domestic building because the problem is usually less acute in rural areas as the architectural quality of the building increases. The formal quality of the manor house or some other major home imposes a discipline which is more easily recognizable and impresses itself even upon those with little sense of architectural history. But in an area which has never known consistent affluence these buildings are few and they tend to be the occasional gems in a village, rather than a major contribution to the structure of a village street. It is also likely that alterations to a building of this sort will be more frequently in the hands of architects and, since many of them are also listed buildings, it is possible to attempt a degree of control over their visual future which is not possible in normal Derbyshire circumstances.

I have already referred to the problem of shape and mass and I have likened the individual rural building to a bead in a necklace. One of the important characteristics of the Derbyshire landscape, and an issue of some importance in rural planning generally is the incidence of minor buildings, of barns and farms which are scattered across the countryside. They belong to an era of small scale farming and they are an echo of an agricultural pattern which is fast disappearing: but they are, nevertheless, part of a well-defined inheritance which we have come to expect in the countryside just as the shelter belts of trees, planted a century or more ago, are an essential complement to the buildings themselves.

The form of the house, the relationship between the house and the barn, the grouping of outbuildings and the whole sense of uniformity which is created by the narrow span buildings of similar materials, all with the same pitch of roof, creates a harmony which we accept readily without the feeling of intrusion. It is interesting that this pattern of building is completely alien to the whole view of modern rural planning where we now talk of limiting building to within the curtilage of existing villages and we try hard to avoid the sprinkling of new building across the landscape. The lack of an accepted vernacular style today is largely responsible for this attitude, but in some areas this has led to a policy where isolated stone structures are allowed to become ruinous so that the population can be assembled within recognizable communities. There are good supporting arguments in favour of this, too, concerned with the availability of social services. There is, however, a difference between maintaining a familiar landscape with buildings as part *of* that landscape and recognizing the cohesion of a village and the grouping of buildings within that village. The isolated building is part of the necklace. It is like a heap of stones with a more organized form: it rises out of the field pattern and the pattern of walls, so it is linked and not, in a landscape sense, an isolated incident. By contrast, the village is composed not usually of entirely isolated houses, but of houses linked in a terrace and with a relationship with the street or a space, which may be the village green or simply an ill-defined amorphous street which is direct and fairly positive or at least sufficient to define the village. Here the grouping of buildings has significance, even though the enclosure of space may be quite loose and arbitrary and in sum quite discontinuous. Rural spaces are informal. They are not controlled tightly by buildings.

Many people have studied the village concept and have looked at the relationship between buildings and landscape, between edges and routes and have sought to explore and define the informality, the intangible qualities which make many villages appear so attractive. When the early planners started to look at the physical structure of communities it is notable that Raymond Unwin particularly turned to the informal romantic English village for inspiration, only to find the village is distinct and particular, it is a collection of buildings around a space or lining a street; it is rarely an experience in depth where you move layer by layer from the centre to the perimeter.[2] The village is skin deep: behind each building there is a garden and often beyond that garden nothing more than fields and open country. Unwin's view of the grouping of buildings is continued by the work of Thomas Sharp, particularly in *The Anatomy of the Village*[3] which explores the whole idea of the spaces inside several seemingly amorphous, informal, communities; but while it is possible to analyze existing examples, the re-creation of villages is elusive and one is forced to conclude that the village really defies final analysis, although that need not mean that it defies extension. The clues have been frequently explored and the root of the village idea is usually to be found in its particular setting. Once again it is a piece of built development growing out of a particular topography.

PROBLEMS OF VILLAGE EXPANSION

It is easier, then, to say what does not, apparently, work in terms of village extension. Here there seems to be almost an ideological concept. Village extensions, as they are practised at the moment, are of two kinds and Derbyshire presents no exception. First, there is that carried out by the local authority for local housing needs. Usually it is done with some sense of social purpose, although often without much imaginative concept of layout. The architect tries hard with the house itself and, so far as the housing manuals and the yardsticks let him, he attempts to produce a well-designed group of buildings, free from the speculator's desire for gimmicks and variety and, because he is working in an area remote from the town, it is likely that his ideas will be modest and somewhat traditionally minded. There are few rural housing schemes anywhere in Britain to equal Tayler and Green's work in Norfolk. Derbyshire, during the 1950s and early 1960s produced a number of small scale housing estates, particularly in Bakewell Rural District which well demonstrated how a conservative view of building design and a clear understanding of simple building techniques is likely to be more acceptable through its deliberate low key approach than many less well controlled modern designs.[4] The trouble is that we so rarely produce as good a modern vernacular like that of Tayler and Green. Where these early designs fail most is in the siting of the buildings in relation to each other: their architects were too keen to use the right-angle and to site quite suitable terraces in parallel rows and they lacked the technique to shape the development properly to the landscape or to create the sort of informal spaces which the existing village pattern usually suggests. When, one might ask, will there be a modern village green?

The speculative village extension is an entirely different matter. The developer aims at a commuting market or at retirement homes: both require variety. Either way he is seeking to house people whose experience of living is usually urban and who seem to want their own traditional town patterns repeated in the countryside. The speculative developer, therefore, has different motives from the local authority. He sees the village as a starting point rather than as a conclusion. Its image will attract his customers, not because they seek the mixture as before but because villages are identifiably nice places to live in or, as it usually works out, nice places to live beside rather than actively to join in socially. These people seem to want associated separateness, detached boxes with close-up views of each other and distant prospects, if possible, of the countryside. But the physical relationship with the village is missing both in fact and in spirit. It is clearly rural suburbia and its manifestation is much more nearly related to the town than to the village. As a phenomenon, therefore, there seems good argument for suggesting that it should be curtailed both in the interest of the physical fabric and also of the social structure of rural communities (Plate 30).

The Peak has had more than its fair share of this type of expansion. There are major estates at Bakewell and Hathersage, smaller new communities at Grindleford and Curbar and an excellent example of how not to expand a village at Great Longstone. The sort of controls that the National Park has exercised do not in fact seem to have done a great deal to create a rural architectural policy. The control of silhouette, of mass, shape and colour is difficult to achieve and the suggestion of pitched roofs and natural stone, or its nearest imitation in colour, still leaves the developer free to interpret his urban housing types simply within the narrow terms of the special rules and the spirit of the control is ignored. The planning of speculative housing has been uniformly bad and has positively injured the landscape as well as many villages.

The speculative village extension demonstrates very well one additional point. This is the impact of the road engineers' approach to layout, not only in the design of the roads themselves but in the design of the details that go with them and the impact their views have upon spatial relationships. The new estates tend to have standard curbs, suburban pavements and small front gardens with standard metal gates from builders' catalogues set uncomfortably in selfconscious stone walls—a mere sop—and the whole relationship of the house to the street and the street to the space between buildings is destroyed. The buildings, in fact, do not group around any space at all and the idea of extending the original character, be it linear or static, using the traditional detailing of floorscape is rarely considered.

The effect of road engineering design has begun to creep into the village itself and traditional surfaces and edges are replaced by standard details. Small areas of grass are removed because of upkeep problems and gradually the floorscape of the village is eroded and uniform, anonymous details in non-traditional materials take their place. To this, of course, may be added the intrusion of new standard signs and street furniture, the addition of standard street lighting both to please the urban residents who are not used to the darkness of the country and to make roads and their junctions safe for motor traffic.

BROAD SCALE CONSERVATION

If, then, we turn away from detail design again to talk of broad landscape conservation this anti-rural tendency at policy level is quite antagonistic to the whole idea of conservation, because the new techniques and standards go a long way towards creating a uniformity in the countryside or the village. Suburban criteria and the gradual erosion of rural quirks and peculiarities are contrary to my view of conservation.

It is not simply that the motor car will only turn on standard radial curves: it is the standardization of urban details within the countryside, the uniformity of site lines and the monotony of regularly placed sodium light standards, the predictability of tarmacadam and regular rhythm of concrete pavings. The road engineer at another level also has the difficult task of dealing with the major through-routes where they cross the Park. Take, for example, the A6 trunk road. This follows the river valley from Matlock to Bakewell and then climbs over the hills to Buxton and away north-west to Stockport and Manchester. It is a source of constant complaint that over the years its character has changed. There are two miniscule stretches of dual carriageway, one near Haddon Hall and the other in Taddingtondale and there are a series of alterations in progress at the moment to iron out a few bends that are considered undesirable and to speed up the flow of traffic generally. It is questionable whether this is desirable and it is doubtful whether money is well spent on reorganizing a whole valley bottom for so little immediate advantage and perhaps it may be in the long term irrelevant. The total positive value may be in the retention of a traditional craft skill through the employment it gives to masons who have constructed several miles of beautiful—but too high—limestone dry walling. But this is a strange price to pay for a dubious improvement and there are many local people who would see the whole thing as retrogressive, particularly when stretches of the river have been artificially re-aligned.

There are other problems, too, where, for example, the A6 passes through built-up areas and the small town of Bakewell is certainly no exception. Here the road is obliged to cross the centre of the town: it enters through two well-defined built-up streets and it passes in front of the principal hotel in the town, the Rutland Arms. Few would disagree that the traffic generated is undesirable, that the shopping streets are made unpleasant with the fumes and noise of big vehicles. But the steps which have been taken to alleviate these problems have, first of all, altered the character of at least one street through ill-advised street widening, and the gradual process of demolition has removed buildings of just the vernacular character which I have described and, of course, destroyed the sense of space and enclosure. In the long run, it may only be a palliative when the issues of where the traffic should go ultimately are under discussion. There has already been, for example, a disastrous proposal mooted for carrying a by-pass through the most sensitive part of the river valley at Bakewell while there are perhaps long-term alternative solutions by re-routing major A6 traffic to the south by upland roads where the environmental damage may be far less drastic. Whatever happens the problems for Bakewell will remain, not so much in the handling of traffic but in the spaces and streets which may have been unnecessarily destroyed. It is sad that you cannot put back the fabric of a small town if you change your mind, and that is a fact which should influence broader decisions before it is too late.

The problem of the A6 should be tackled at a more radical level which appraises the whole road pattern for the Park and places it in a regional context. This must take account of the motorway networks of the country as a whole and the discussions as well as the mysteries surrounding the projected trans-Pennine route between Sheffield and Manchester are not irrelevant. May be it will be sensible to accept a major motorway link north or south of the Park in order to relieve internal roads within the Park itself. These are grand concepts which may not take place for many years and while the debate goes on the A6 and other roads, too, are constantly the subject of alterations and so-called improvements while towns like Bakewell continue to be at risk.

It is necessary, therefore, to challenge the process of decision making which lies behind county as well as Ministry road proposals and to question the validity of seemingly piecemeal decisions which are so clearly not in the interests of conservation. If Bakewell is eroded then one of the most attractive towns in the Park will have suffered irrevocably and if the valley which contains the A6 is redesigned much further we shall be dealing with man-made environment at a scale which is alien to that of the landscape. What is the price of a few lost minutes on a journey by contrast with the cost of a mile or two of new road, let alone of motorway?

Conclusion

Derbyshire and the Peak Park are a microcosm. The problem of conservation is not simply defined in a rural area and one view of it should encompass the tactics of regional planning as well as the education of ordinary people about window design. It cannot be seen as an isolated policy of preservation and I hope I have demonstrated that in a national park, where the preservation of the existing quality of environment is ranked as a fundamental priority, it is still an issue more concerned with future policies, with local livelihood and above all with a belief that conservation is a positive way of life and one which is in the common interest. The conservation of ordinariness is an elusive proposal, but a realistic one if this delicate built fabric is to go on providing a memorable landscape of which it is a significant part and of which it has its whole being.

NOTES AND REFERENCES

1 *Peak District National Park Development Plan, First Review, Report and Analysis of Survey*, Buxton, Peak Park Planning Board, 1966, p. 19.
2 Parker, Barry and Unwin, Raymond, *The Art of Building a Home*, London Longmans, 1901.
3 Sharp, Thomas, *The Anatomy of the Village*, Harmondsworth, Penguin, 1946.
4 There are examples of this kind of council housing near Calver, at Earl Sterndale and Great Longstone.

Conservation reports and studies

A bibliographic note

ROBIN BLOXSIDGE

Local authority work on the preservation of individual buildings, with the conservation of areas of towns and villages and of landscapes, rarely becomes general knowledge. The attention received by the problems of Norwich, Chester, Edinburgh and so on is exceptional; and it is so because the problems of such cities are exceptional, principally because of the large number of buildings of architectural and historical interest which they retain and which reduce the scope for physical change in urban evolution and planning. However, almost every town and village has at least one building, if not a group of buildings or area, worthy of conservation. The list which follows and this preamble to it, constitute an attempt to note some of the problems encountered by local authorities in planning for conservation and at the same time to bring to the notice of a wide audience the considerable amount of work which local planning authorities have done and are continuing to do.

In 1975 requests were sent by the *Town Planning Review* to Chief Planning Officers in England and Wales for copies of conservation reports they had prepared. This exercise was repeated in 1976 and this time Scotland and Northern Ireland were included.[1] They are listed, with addresses for enquiry as to the details of their price and availability, below. The length of the list is indicative not only of the sheer volume of work in hand, but of the very widespread response to the request for reports. The response was, in fact, much greater, and the *Review* is extremely grateful to those planning authorities which sent reports and equally to those who wrote lengthy and helpful letters or whose officers engaged in useful telephone conversations with editorial staff. Letters were received from more than 50% and reports from a third. The reports were put on exhibition in the University of Liverpool in October and have now been placed in the University library, in the Department of Civic Design. Some points about the number and scope of the reports are worth making, in the light of the interesting comments put forward in letters received from local authorities.

Unless it is dealing with individual buildings, most conservation planning starts with the designation of a conservation area. It is notable that the majority of the publications and other documents listed below are reports or public consultation leaflets dealing with designation, which is only a first stage in the conservation process. The number presented represents only a small proportion of the designations which have taken place and which are being made almost daily. A large number of the new district authorities are continuing to concentrate on designation rather than on plans for enhancement. Many of these authorities have made the point that this initial step (easier to take under the 1974 Act than it was previously) at least affords the benefits of extra development control protection to many areas and is, therefore, an essential first step in conservation. Some authorities are unable to proceed to this stage, and others are unable to advance to the stage of positive planning, for various reasons.

One of the principal reasons put forward for lack of activity is shortage of staff. It was widely predicted at the time of local government reorganization that the two-tier system of planning responsibility would lead to staff shortage and this is now apparent. Twelve months since reorganization have passed at the time of writing (May 1975), and still a large number of local planning departments are only now completing their staffing arrangements; many posts in smaller authorities especially remain unfilled. This is a problem which can only be resolved in time, as the training of more planners continues. More serious at present is the effect of financial cuts in local authority expenditure, which are causing many posts to remain unfilled. Such economies are also responsible in a large number of cases for the absence of reports on conservation areas. It is not, after all, essential to produce glossy brochures or reports in the designation stage, although it could be argued cogently that such publications are likely to strengthen public awareness, interest and support. An advertisement in the local newspaper is not the best way to excite imagination! There, is however, very often no way round a halt to report production in the present economic situation; many planning officers' letters emphasized their small budgets. The absence of a listing below for some areas, therefore, does not mean that the local planning authorities are idle—they may, indeed, be very active. This may well mean that they have, despite problems of finding staff and of paying them, found ways round the staffing problems.

Most usually, staffing difficulties are overcome by cooperation between district and county authorities, so that the special skills and expertise can be shared. Such an arrangement can lead to the formation of one centralized conservation team working throughout a county, or of district teams staffed from county and district planning departments. In the latter case, the teams may be permanent or they may come together for a specific project. In some counties, most of the conservation work has continued to be done at county level where the necessary skills were to be found and some districts will start doing their own work as and when they have the financial and personnel resources to do so. Less rarely, county staff are deployed in the district, but are under the supervision of the district planning officer rather than of their employer. Sometimes, county staff will simply be available to advise newly-formed conservation teams. In these ways, and in others, county and district authorities are cooperating in conservation planning.

The same kind of cooperation is evident in the production and operation of 'town schemes', which allow for finance to be provided for conservation improvements. Grant aid under a town scheme is met 50 per cent by the government and 50 per cent by a local authority. The local money may sometimes be provided jointly by a district and a county authority. Town schemes are not, however, numerous, as Honor Chapman has pointed out in her chapter, and this is reflected in the few examples of leaflets listed below.

The listing of reports received is generally by the authority which provided them and, thus, does not always indicate their authorship or show where reports are cooperative ventures. A large number of the reports available from districts are, in fact, the result of work before local government reorganization by county authorities; in the first year of their existence the new district authorities could not be expected to accomplish a very great deal. Some planning departments have made use of consultants and in many cases this is shown in the list. The employment of consultants is obviously a very easy way around the problem of the scarcity of planners expert in the field of conservation.

Another feature of the reports received is the small proportion which are angled towards a positive plan for enhancement of conservation areas. The proportion of these among those most recently produced is, however, much higher than it was two or three years ago. This reflects a new emphasis by authorities whose concentrated efforts on designation since 1967 are now coming to an end. It also mirrors the spirit of the new (1974) legislation. Plans for enhancement do, of course, demand finance and they are, more than designations, subject to cuts in local authority expenditure. Absence of enhancement plans does not necessarily mean that they do not exist. Some authorities have said that they have finished, or are finishing, their designation programmes and will now concentrate on enhancement. They will not, however, always publish reports for this purpose.

Some of the most interesting and imaginatively produced publications are those specially for EAHY. Common forms taken by these are booklets about local buildings or 'trails', both of which have been produced in novel and interesting ways. They comprise an effort which, if sustained, can play a considerable part in increasing the awareness of architectural heritage. It is, perhaps, invidious to single out one authority, but the list of imaginative material shown for Staffordshire County Council is surely unique.

While the work of local authorities in conservation practice has been considerable, it does not represent the total effort being made. As well as a growing effort being made by private individuals and groups and by industrial and commercial concerns, voluntary organizations have become involved in conservation planning. This ensures that the environment will be cared for as a matter of public, rather than political, concern. Not only are the amenity societies interested, but other organizations, such as Councils of Social Service, are now playing a part—often taking a leading role. It is the duty of local authorities to encourage this involvement and the new Heritage Bureaux are valuable forums for a new cooperative spirit in conservation planning.

The involvement of all kinds of groups and societies, and the valuable educational function they can play, are vital. So, too, is the continuing interest beyond Heritage Year of schools and colleges. In this area of planning, more than in any other, education and the awakening of public interest are essential to build on the successes already achieved.

NOTE

1 In Northern Ireland, conservation areas are the responsibility of the Department of the Environment (NI) which is the local planning agency for Northern Ireland. It operates its planning service through six divisional offices.

Chester

Chester: The Victorian Clock Tower, a landmark on the City Walls at Eastgate
(Photograph: Donald Insall and Associates)

Chester

2 Above: Eastgate Street, the principal Shopping
Street in Chester showing the Shops of various
sizes at ground level. A unique feature is that
shopping also takes place in the Rows at the first
floor level (photograph: Chester Chronicle)

*These buildings have been restored with the
aid of government grants and show how
meticulous attention has been paid to detail.
The Dutch Houses and 49 Bridge Street Row
received Civic Trust Heritage Year Awards
for restoration work*

3 Chester: The Dutch Houses in Bridge Street
(photograph: Civic Trust)

27 Derbyshire:
stone detailing on a barn;
limestone walling with
gritstone details

Derbyshire: the walled fields of the limestone plateau which it has been suggested
should be included as a national heritage area

Derbyshire

29   Derbyshire: a traditional house, rendered and with a careful extension to the left

30   Derbyshire: housing in a rural area, incorporating suburban features which are out of character with the Derbyshire heritage